10

MINUTE GUIDE TO

COREL WORDPERFECT 7® FOR WINDOWS® 95

by Barbara Kasser

A Division of Macmillan Computer Publishing
201 West 103rd St., Indianapolis, Indiana 46290 USA

To my husband Bill and my son Richard who add the sunshine to my life. I love you, guys.

©1996 by Que® Corporation

Library of Congress Catalog Card Number: 95-72558
International Standard Book Number: 0-7897-0454-4

98 97 96   8 7 6 5 4 3 2 1

Interpretation of the printing code: the rightmost double-digit number is the year of the book's first printing; the rightmost single-digit number is the number of the book's printing. For example, a printing code of 96-1 shows that this copy of the book was printed during the first printing of the book in 1996.

Printed in the United States of America

Publisher *Roland Elgey*

Vice President and Publisher *Marie Butler-Knight*

Publishing Manager *Lynn E. Zingraf*

Editorial Services Director *Elizabeth Keaffaber*

Managing Editor *Michael Cunningham*

Acquisitions Editor *Martha O'Sullivan*

Product Development Specialist *Melanie Palaisa*

Production Editor *Audra Gable*

Book Designer *Barbara Kordesh*

Cover Designer *Dan Armstrong*

Indexer *Chris Wilcox*

Production *Marcia Brizendine, Terri Edwards, Bryan Flores, Trey Frank, DiMonique Ford, Damon Jordan, Paul Wilson*

Special thanks to Herb Feltner for ensuring the technical accuracy of this book.

Contents

1 STARTING AND EXITING WORDPERFECT FOR WINDOWS 95   **1**

Parts of the WordPerfect Screen 1
Exiting WordPerfect 3

2 USING WORDPERFECT'S TOOLS   **5**

Using the Menu Bar 5
Using the Toolbar 7
Using the Power Bar 10
Using the Ruler Bar 11
Working with WordPerfect Dialog Boxes 12

3 USING ONLINE HELP   **15**

Using the Help Menu 15
The Help Topics Screen 16
Using Ask the PerfectExpert 19
Using QuickTips 20

4 CREATING A NEW DOCUMENT   **22**

Creating a Document from Scratch 22
Starting a New Document with a Template 23
Entering Text 26
Moving Around in a Document 27
Changing the Screen View 30

5 EDITING TEXT   **32**

Inserting Text 32
Typing over Existing Text 32
Correcting That Oops! 33
Undoing Your Changes 36

6 WORKING WITH BLOCKS OF TEXT   **39**

Selecting Text Blocks 39
Deleting a Text Block 42
Copying and Moving Text Blocks 42

7 SAVING AND CLOSING DOCUMENTS 46

Saving a Document 46
Using the Save As Command 48
Closing a File 50

8 RETRIEVING DOCUMENTS 51

Opening Existing Documents 51
Finding a File Using QuickFinder 55
Viewing Multiple Documents 57

9 PRINTING YOUR DOCUMENT 59

Getting Ready to Print 59
Previewing Your Document Before You Print 61
Printing Your Document 62
Using the Make It Fit Expert 64
Using Binding and Two-Sided Printing 65

10 CREATING ENVELOPES AND LABELS 68

Creating Envelopes 68
Working with Labels 71

11 WORKING WITH WORDPERFECT CODES 75

What Are WordPerfect Codes? 75
Revealing Hidden Codes 77
Removing Codes 79
Changing Codes.. 80

12 CHANGING THE APPEARANCE OF YOUR TEXT 81

Character Formatting.. 81
Changing the Font Size or Attributes of Text 82
Changing the Default Font 83
Applying Attributes Using the Power Bar
    and the Toolbar 85

13 SETTING THE LINE SPACING AND JUSTIFICATION 87

Changing Line Spacing 87
Understanding Justification 88
Changing Justification in a Document 89

14 SETTING TABS   **91**

What Are Tabs? 91
Viewing the Tab Stop Settings 92
Types of Tab Stops 92
Clearing Tab Stops 93
Changing Tab Settings 94

15 PARAGRAPH FORMATTING   **98**

What Is a Paragraph? 98
Using Indents 99
Using QuickSpots 101
Using QuickFormat 102

16 SETTING THE PAGE SIZE AND MARGINS   **104**

Selecting the Page Size 104
Setting Page Margins 107

**17 WORKING WITH PAGE NUMBERS,
     HEADERS, AND FOOTERS**   **110**

Adding Page Numbers 110
Controlling Page Breaks 112
What Are Headers and Footers? 113
Creating Headers and Footers 114
Editing a Header or Footer 116
Turning Off Headers and Footers 117

18 CREATING NUMBERED AND BULLETED LISTS   **118**

Creating a Bulleted or Numbered List 118
Adding Items to and Removing Items from a
    Numbered List 120

19 CREATING COLUMNS   **122**

Understanding WordPerfect Columns 122
Defining Columns in Your Document 124

20   Working with Tables   127

What Is a Table? 127
Creating a Table 128
Moving Around and Typing Text in a Table 129
Changing the Table's Size and Appearance 130
Numbers Options 134
Summing a Table Column 134

21   Dressing Up Your Document   135

Adding a Drop Cap 135
Using WordPerfect Characters 137
Centering Text on a Page 138
Adding a Border 139

22   Finding and Replacing Text   143

Finding a Text String 143
Replacing Text or Codes 146

23   Using WordPerfect's Writing Tools   150

Checking Your Spelling 150
Checking Your Grammar 153
Using the Thesaurus 154

**24   Adding Graphic Objects to
       Your Document   157**

Adding Pictures to Your Document 157
Using TextArt 161
Adding Graphic Lines to Your Document 163
Using Watermarks 163

25   Using Internet Publisher   166

What Is the Internet? 166
Creating a Web Document 167
Publishing to HTML 171
Launching the Netscape Navigator Browser 172

Index   173

Introduction

Congratulations! You've made the decision to learn WordPerfect for Windows 95, the world's best word processing program. WordPerfect has been helping computer users create perfect documents since the mid-1980s. Today, Corel WordPerfect 7 for Windows 95 contains a collection of powerful features and options that elevate the program to a new level.

Because you don't have time to thumb through the manual that came with WordPerfect each time you want to learn how to do something new, you need a simple book that provides the techniques and steps to get you working. You don't need thick manuals that fill your head with extra information.

Relax. After a few brief lessons in this book, you'll be on your way to becoming a WordPerfect superstar!

Welcome to the *10 Minute* Guide to Corel WordPerfect 7 for Windows 95

Where do you start? What do you need to know? How can you get up and running quickly? The 10 Minute Guide focuses on WordPerfect's most often used features. This book does not attempt to teach you everything about the program. Instead, it concentrates only on the things you need to know.

This 10 Minute Guide teaches you about WordPerfect for Windows 95 without using confusing terms and technical jargon. The straightforward explanations are easy to understand, and the numbered steps tell you which option to select and which keys to press. Each lesson is self-contained and should take 10 minutes or less to complete.

Why You Need This Book

The *10 Minute Guide to Corel WordPerfect 7 for Windows 95* is for anyone who:

- Wants to become proficient with WordPerfect for Windows 95 quickly

- Feels overwhelmed or frightened by the complexity of WordPerfect

- Needs to learn the steps necessary to complete particular tasks

- Wants a clear, plain-English guide that details the main features of WordPerfect

How This Book Is Organized

The *10 Minute Guide to Corel WordPerfect 7 for Windows 95* consists of a series of self-contained lessons that you can follow in sequential order. If this is your first encounter with WordPerfect for Windows, start with Lesson 1 and work through Lesson 10 in order. These lessons lead you through the process of creating, editing, printing, and saving a document. If you have some WordPerfect experience, you might want to jump ahead to the lessons that discuss the features you want to learn about.

If WordPerfect for Windows 95 is not installed on your computer, consult the inside front cover for installation instructions.

This book is designed for someone who has used a computer before, either at work or at home. You should already know the basic skills of using the mouse and keyboard. While you may not be familiar with WordPerfect or Windows 95, you probably have worked with some other computer programs or games.

ICONS AND CONVENTIONS USED IN THIS BOOK

You'll find the following conventions used throughout the book
to help you know what you're supposed to do:

What you type	Things you need to type appear in bold blue type.
Press Enter	Keys you are to press and items you are to select appear in blue type.
On-screen text	On-screen messages appear in bold type.
Press Alt+F1	Key combinations you must press simultaneously appear in this format. This means that you press and hold the first key (in this case, the Alt key) and then press the second key (F1). Then you release both keys.

You'll also find the following icons throughout this book. They
mark information intended to help you save time and to teach
you important information fast.

 Timesaver Tip icons point out hints and shortcuts for using the program more efficiently.

 Plain English icons mark explanations of new terms.

 Panic Button icons identify information that can help you avoid trouble—or help you get out of trouble you're already in.

ACKNOWLEDGMENTS

Thanks to everyone at Que who helped with this book—especially Martha O'Sullivan, Stephanie Gould, Herb Feltner, and most of all, Melanie Palaisa and Audra Gable.

TRADEMARKS

All terms mentioned in this book that are known to be trademarks have been appropriately capitalized. Que cannot attest to the accuracy of this information. Use of a term in this book should not be regarded as affecting the validity of any trademark or service mark.

STARTING AND EXITING WORDPERFECT FOR WINDOWS 95

In this lesson, you will learn how to start and exit WordPerfect for Windows 95. You'll also learn about the parts of the WordPerfect screen.

Windows 95 must be up and running on your computer before you can start WordPerfect for Windows 95. Follow these steps to start WordPerfect:

1. Click the Start button and select Corel WordPerfect Suite 7.

2. Select WordPerfect 7, and the WordPerfect window opens.

PARTS OF THE WORDPERFECT SCREEN

Figure 1.1 shows the WordPerfect document screen. The WordPerfect screen consists of the elements and tools as described in the list below.

Title bar Displays the name of the program that's running (WordPerfect) and the name of the active document. If you haven't saved the open document yet, a generic name (such as Document1) appears.

Maximize, Minimize/Restore and Close Buttons
Windows 95 control buttons. Click the Close (X) button to exit WordPerfect. The Maximize/Restore button functions as a toggle; click it once to expand the WordPerfect screen to its full size, and click it again to restore the WordPerfect

screen to its previous size. Click the Minimize button to shrink the window to a button on the taskbar.

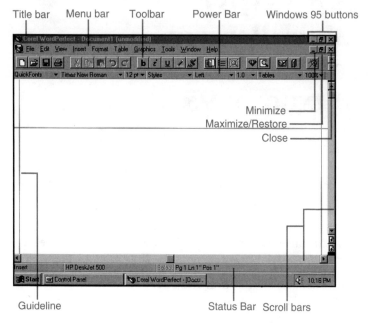

FIGURE 1.1 The WordPerfect document screen is where it all starts.

Menu bar Displays a list of drop-down menus. Each menu contains a list of related commands (see Lesson 2).

Toolbar Contains buttons for quick access to common tasks. WordPerfect has several Toolbars available (see Lesson 2).

Power Bar Provides buttons to help you format your WordPerfect document (see Lessons 2 and 12).

Document screen The main part of the screen, in which you type your document.

Cursor The small vertical blinking line. Text you type appears to the right of the cursor.

Guidelines   Colored lines that define the left, right, top, and bottom margins on the document screen. (You might need to turn these on through the View menu.)

Scroll bar   Enables you to move through a document that is too long or too wide to fit on the screen. Use the vertical scroll bar to move up and down through your document; use the horizontal scroll bar to move to the right and left.

Status Bar   Provides system information, such as the currently selected printer, the typing mode, and the position of the cursor. Double-click a Status Bar button to access the related feature quickly.

Windows 95 taskbar   Appears in all Windows 95 applications. Consult your Windows documentation for more information about the taskbar.

A Helping Hand   Anytime you need help in WordPerfect, TIP   press F1 to access online Help. See Lesson 3 for details about using Help.

EXITING WORDPERFECT

When you finish working in WordPerfect, you should close the program using either of the following methods:

- Open the File menu and choose Exit.

- Click the Close (X) button in the upper-right corner of the WordPerfect screen.

If you've made changes to a document that you haven't saved, WordPerfect shows a dialog box asking if you want to save that file. If you want to close the file without saving it, answer No. (If you want to save the file, skip to Lesson 7.)

TIP **Minimize** If you're done working in WordPerfect for right now but you plan to come back to the program soon, consider minimizing it instead of closing it. Click the Minimize button to collapse WordPerfect to the Windows 95 taskbar. When you're ready to restore the program to the screen, click the WordPerfect button on the taskbar.

In this lesson, you learned how to open WordPerfect. You also learned about parts of the WordPerfect screen. In the next lesson, you'll learn how to use WordPerfect's tools to help you create a document.

USING WORDPERFECT'S TOOLS

In this lesson you'll learn how to use WordPerfect's menu bar, Toolbar, Power Bar, and Ruler Bar. You'll also learn how to work with dialog boxes.

USING THE MENU BAR

The menu bar always appears at the top of the screen, as shown in Figure 2.1. You can access all of WordPerfect's features through the layers of menus it provides. Each word in the menu bar represents a menu full of commands from which you can choose to tell WordPerfect what you want to do.

Menu bar ——

Power Bar ——

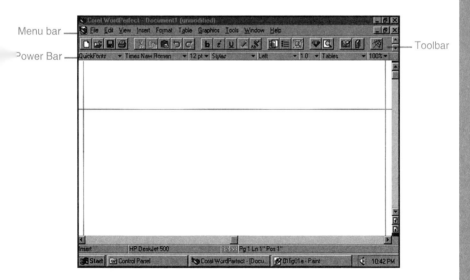

—— Toolbar

FIGURE 2.1 WordPerfect provides many tools intended to make your job easier.

To activate one of the menus, click the menu name you want and drag the mouse pointer down to (or just click) the selection you want to use. As you will see, some menu commands have little symbols next to them. When you work with the menu commands, you'll need to know the following symbols:

Right arrow   A right arrow represents a submenu of additional commands from which to choose. When you select the command with the arrow, the submenu appears. To select a command on the submenu, you drag the mouse to that command and click.

Ellipsis   An ellipsis (...) after a menu item indicates that if you select that command, a dialog box will appear from which you can choose options about the menu command or enter more information.

Check mark   A check mark in front of a command means that the option is turned on. You can toggle this kind of option on and off by clicking the command. When the check mark is visible (the option is on), you click the item to turn it off, and the check mark disappears. Click an option that does not have a check mark (it's turned off), and the check mark appears.

Plain command   If a menu item does not have a symbol next to it, choosing the item implements the action related to the menu command. For example, if you choose View, Reveal Codes, WordPerfect displays the Reveal Codes window.

Shortcut key   A keystroke or combination of keys that activates a command without you having to choose it from the menu. Not all menu commands have shortcut key equivalents.

Dimmed commands   If a menu item is dimmed or grayed out, the command is currently unavailable. (A command might be unavailable, for example, if you have not given WordPerfect enough information to perform that command.)

If you accidentally open a menu, or if you decide that you don't want to use the menu when it is open on-screen, move the mouse pointer off the menu and click. The menu automatically closes.

Using the Toolbar

Directly below the menu bar is the WordPerfect Toolbar (see Figure 2.1). The Toolbar contains small squares called *buttons*. These buttons are shortcuts to many commonly used functions that can also be accessed through the menu bar. For example, the Print button offers a shortcut for the File Print command. Clicking the Print Toolbar button to print a document is much faster than finding the Print menu command.

WordPerfect provides a number of other Toolbars, which are customized for specific tasks such as editing, formatting, and working with graphics. The WordPerfect 7 Toolbar is the standard Toolbar (the one that appears automatically) and contains buttons used for general tasks. You'll learn to switch to or display other Toolbars later in this lesson.

Where's My Regular Toolbar? When you select certain program options, WordPerfect replaces your current Toolbar with the one that goes along with the feature you've chosen. When you finish with that feature, the standard WordPerfect 7 Toolbar is restored.

You can move the Toolbar so that it appears in a different place on the screen, and you can even remove it from the screen completely. You'll learn how to do both later in this lesson.

Toolbar Quick Reference The inside back cover of this book shows the buttons on the WordPerfect 7 Toolbar. You'll learn how to use many of these buttons in later lessons.

SWITCHING TO ANOTHER TOOLBAR

Although the WordPerfect 7 Toolbar is set as a default, WordPerfect comes with many other Toolbars you can display. For example, if you are creating a document that contains graphic images, you might want to select the Graphics Toolbar, which contains buttons for the commands used most often when working with graphics.

You can change the Toolbar by following these steps:

1. Position the mouse pointer over any button on the Toolbar.

2. Click the *right* mouse button.

3. Select a new Toolbar name from the list that appears.

 Right-Click When you place the mouse pointer over an object and click the right mouse button, a shortcut menu appears showing commands specific to that object. Right-clicking is used extensively in Windows 95.

MOVING THE TOOLBAR

No matter which Toolbar is displayed, you can relocate it to any area of the screen or resize it as necessary to fit your needs. To place the Toolbar at the bottom of the screen or along the left or right side, place the mouse pointer on a blank area of the Toolbar. The mouse pointer takes the shape of a hand. Drag the Toolbar to the left, right, or bottom of the screen. As you drag, an outline of the Toolbar moves with the mouse pointer. Release the mouse button, and the Toolbar appears in its new location.

Take It Away   To hide the Toolbar, select View, Toolbars/Ruler and click the check box next to WordPerfect 7 Toolbar. When you want to redisplay the Toolbar, repeat that command sequence (which toggles the Toolbar display back on).

You can also place the Toolbar in the *document window* itself. To do so, click a blank area of the Toolbar and drag to the desired location. When you release the mouse button, the Toolbar becomes an adjustable rectangle called a *palette*. To resize the Toolbar palette after you've moved it into the document window, click any edge of the palette. When the mouse pointer changes to a two-headed arrow, drag until it is the shape you want. When you release the mouse button, WordPerfect rearranges the Toolbar buttons to fit the new rectangle.

Document Window   The main area of the WordPerfect screen, which is where you'll type your text.

DISPLAYING MORE THAN ONE ROW OF TOOLBAR BUTTONS

WordPerfect displays one row of Toolbar buttons by default. You can change the display to show two or more rows of buttons. Take these steps to show multiple rows of Toolbar buttons.

1. Position the mouse pointer over a blank spot on the Toolbar (the mouse pointer turns into a hand) and right-click.

2. Select Preferences from the list that appears, and the Toolbar Preferences dialog box appears.

3. Click Options. WordPerfect displays the Toolbar Options dialog box.

4. In the Maximum Number of rows/columns to show spin box, increase the number to 2 or more.

5. Click OK to close the Toolbar Options dialog box, and then click Close to close the Toolbar Preferences dialog box and return to the document screen. The Toolbar now displays two rows of buttons.

> **TIP** **More Buttons!** The WordPerfect 7 Toolbar contains more buttons than can fit across the top of the screen. To view all of the buttons at once, move the Toolbar into the document window or expand the Toolbar to two rows.

USING THE POWER BAR

The Power Bar is below the WordPerfect 7 Toolbar. It provides you with a quick way to make formatting changes (changes to the font and the size of text, for example) to your document. Unlike the Toolbar, the Power Bar does not change when you access any of WordPerfect's features.

Table 2.1 lists the Power Bar buttons and their functions. To use the Power Bar, click one of its buttons to open the associated drop-down list and then select an item from that list. To make more in-depth changes (for example, to change the line spacing to 3), double-click a button to open its corresponding dialog box.

TABLE 2.1 POWER BAR BUTTONS

BUTTON	FUNCTION
QuickFonts ▼	Displays as many as 20 of the most recently used typefaces
Times New Roman ▼	Changes the typeface of selected text

BUTTON	FUNCTION
12 pt ▼	Changes the size of selected text
Styles ▼	Changes the style of selected text
Left ▼	Changes the alignment of selected text
1.0 ▼	Changes the line spacing of selected text
Tables ▼	Creates a table in the document
100% ▼	Changes the magnification of the active window

USING THE RULER BAR

The Ruler Bar is hidden by default; however, you can display it at the top of your workspace at any time. The Ruler Bar shows the location of the left and right margins, as well as indents and tab settings for the current paragraph.

Figure 2.2 shows the screen with the Ruler Bar displayed. To display the Ruler Bar, open the View menu, choose Toolbars/Ruler, and select Ruler. To hide it again, repeat the steps.

When you have the Ruler Bar turned on, you can drag any margin, indent, or tab stop marker to a new location to change it. To remove a tab stop, drag it downward off the Ruler Bar. You'll learn more about changing margins, indents, and tab settings in Lesson 16.

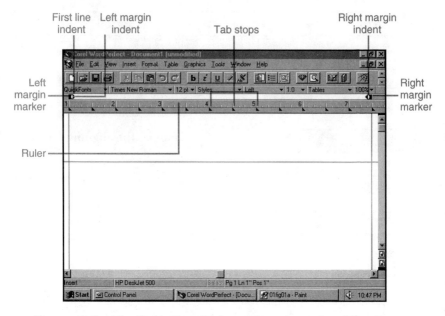

First line indent   Left margin indent   Tab stops   Right margin indent

Left margin marker   Right margin marker

Ruler

FIGURE 2.2   The Ruler Bar displays tab and margin settings.

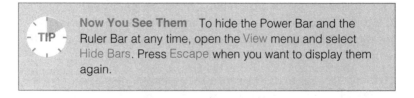

TIP   **Now You See Them**   To hide the Power Bar and the Ruler Bar at any time, open the View menu and select Hide Bars. Press Escape when you want to display them again.

WORKING WITH WORDPERFECT DIALOG BOXES

Anytime you select a command that's followed by an ellipsis (...), WordPerfect for Windows 95 provides a *dialog box*. Think of a dialog box as a form you need to complete and verify for Windows to proceed. Figure 2.3 shows a dialog box and some of its elements.

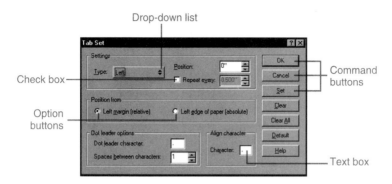

FIGURE 2.3   A typical dialog box.

Each dialog box contains one or more of the following items:

- **Tabs** allow you to look at different "pages" of options. To see a set of related options, click its tab.

- **List boxes** provide two or more available choices. You select the item you want by clicking it.

- **Drop-down lists** show only one item and hide the rest. To view all of the items in the list, click the down arrow to the right of the list box.

- **Text boxes** are like "fill-in-the-blank" boxes. Click inside of a text box to activate it. If there's already text inside the box, use the Delete or Backspace keys to delete existing characters before you type.

- **Check boxes** allow you to turn options on or off. Click inside a check box to turn an option on if it's off (or vice versa). Note that if there are multiple check boxes displayed together, you can select more than one.

- **Spin boxes** are text boxes with controls. To change a spin box's setting, you can either type the new setting in the text box or click the up or down arrow to change it.

- **Command buttons** appear in every dialog box. The most common command buttons are OK, Cancel, and

Help. Click the OK command button to tell WordPerfect to accept all of the options you requested in your dialog box.

- **Option buttons** are a lot like check boxes, except that you can select only one option button in a group. Clicking one button deselects any other option that is already selected.

In this lesson, you learned how to use the Toolbar, Power Bar, and Ruler Bar and how to display and hide them. You also learned how to work with dialog boxes. In the next lesson, you'll learn how to use WordPerfect's online Help system.

USING ONLINE HELP

In this lesson, you'll learn how to use the online Help system. You'll also learn how to ask a question in your own words so the PerfectExpert can guide you through a task.

USING THE HELP MENU

The Help menu gives you access to WordPerfect's online Help system, which provides information on program features, offers step-by-step instructions, and performs tasks for you. The Help menu contains the following five commands:

- **Help Topics** displays the main Help screen, entitled Help Topics: WordPerfect Help.

- **Ask the PerfectExpert** starts the PerfectExpert feature (which you can also access from the Help Topics screen).

- **Help Online** lets you connect to an online information service. This command is available only if your system is configured for an Internet connection.

- **Upgrade Help** displays help for users who have used other versions of WordPerfect or other word processing programs.

- **About Corel WordPerfect** displays information about the WordPerfect for Windows 95 program, including the program version and the license number.

Need Help with Help Online? Refer to your system documentation if you need additional information about connecting to Help Online.

THE HELP TOPICS SCREEN

Click Help on the menu bar and choose Help Topics, and you'll see the Help Topics dialog box shown in Figure 3.1. The Help Topics dialog box contains the Contents, Index, and Find tabs that are standard in Windows 95 programs. In addition, the WordPerfect's Help Topics screen includes a Show Me tab.

FIGURE 3.1   The Help Topics: WordPerfect Help screen.

THE CONTENTS, INDEX, AND FIND TABS

Help Topics provide quick access to a large base of information about WordPerfect. The program information is arranged in several ways so that you can access it in whichever way is best for your situation.

- **Contents** Double-click any entry with a book icon to open it, and entries for sub-books and documents appear. Double-click a sub-book or a document entry to open it.

- **Index** Type the word you want to look up, and the Index list scrolls to that part of the alphabetical listing. When you see the topic in the list that you want to read, double-click it.

- **Find**   The first time you click this tab, Windows tells you it needs to create a list. Click Next to allow it to do so. When it finishes creating the list, click Finish, and you'll see the main Find tab. Type the word you want to find in the top text box. Then click a word in the middle box to narrow the search. Finally, review the list of Help topics at the bottom, and double-click the one you want to read.

THE SHOW ME TAB

The Show Me tab contains many of WordPerfect's most commonly used features. In the Help Topics dialog box, click the Show Me tab to start PerfectExpert. Figure 3.2 shows the Show Me tab.

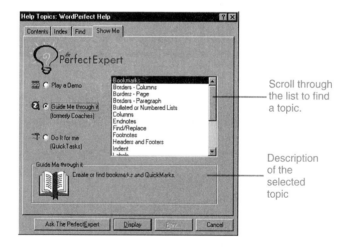

FIGURE 3.2   Select the Show Me tab to start the PerfectExpert feature.

PerfectExpert offers you these three help options:

- **Play a Demo**   Click the Play a Demo button, and then scroll through the topic list and choose a topic. (Make sure that the Corel Suite CD is in your computer's

CD-ROM drive before you select Play a Demo.) Word-Perfect displays a brief movie demonstration for the selected topic. When the movie is over, you are returned to the Help Topics dialog box.

- **Guide Me through it**   Click the Guide Me through it button and select a topic from the list. A brief description appears in the Guide Me through it area at the bottom of the dialog box (see Figure 3.2).

- **Do It for me**   If you want WordPerfect to perform a task for you, click the Do It for me (Quick Tasks) button and select a topic. Follow the on-screen instructions and fill in any information WordPerfect asks for as it completes the task for you. When the task is completed, WordPerfect returns you to the document screen.

If you want more information about the topic you've selected on the right side of the Show Me tab, click the Display button. PerfectExpert shows you more information about your topic, as shown in Figure 3.3. If you want step-by-step guidance for a task, or if you want the PerfectExpert to perform much of the task for you, click the appropriate button. Click the red Stop button to return to the document screen.

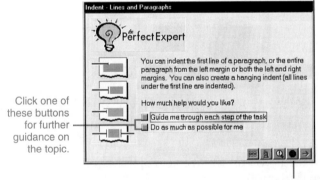

Click one of these buttons for further guidance on the topic.

Click the Stop button to return to the document screen.

FIGURE 3.3   PerfectExpert can guide you through a task or do it for you!

Help Is Only a Keypress Away   If you find that you need help while you're in the middle of a task, press the F1 key, and WordPerfect displays a Help screen to guide you.

USING ASK THE PERFECTEXPERT

WordPerfect's Ask the PerfectExpert feature enables you to ask for help using your own words. For example, you can simply ask "how do I set margins?" just as you would if you were talking to a coworker. In response, the PerfectExpert displays a list of choices related to your topic, as shown in Figure 3.4

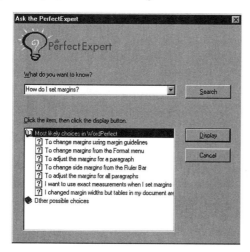

FIGURE 3.4   Ask the PerfectExpert and view the answers.

To use Ask the PerfectExpert, follow these steps:

1. Open the Help menu and select Ask the PerfectExpert. The Ask the PerfectExpert dialog box appears.

2. Type your question in the text box provided. You don't have to type a complete sentence. For example, you can type the word "Margins" to see all of the topics related to margins.

PerfectExpert from the Toolbar   You can also click the Ask the PerfectExpert Toolbar button to access the dialog box. To make the button visible, drag the Toolbar into the document screen or display two rows of Toolbar buttons as described in Lesson 2.

If You've Asked Before...   You can display a list of questions you've asked previously by clicking the down arrow next to the text box in the Ask the PerfectExpert dialog box. Select the question from the list and click Search.

3. Click the Search button, and a list of likely choices appears (see Figure 3.4).

4. Select your choice from the list and click Display to view it. The WordPerfect Help program appears in a separate window on top of the document screen with information about your choice. Click WordPerfect Help's Close (X) button to close the Help window and return to the document screen.

USING QUICKTIPS

QuickTips give you quick answers about the functions of the buttons on the Toolbar, the Power Bar, and the Status Bar, and about various options on the menu bar. When you point to a button for a few seconds, a QuickTips explanation pops up in a balloon next to the pointer, as shown in Figure 3.5.

You can also get QuickTips within dialog boxes. To see an explanation of an item in a dialog box, click the question mark in the upper-right corner of the box and then click the option about which you want help. The QuickTips balloon provides you with a brief description of the item.

QuickTip

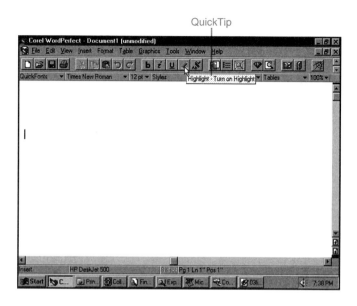

FIGURE 3.5   QuickTips can be very helpful.

By default, the QuickTips feature is turned on. However, you can turn QuickTips off at any time by following these steps:

1. Open the Edit menu and select Preferences.

2. Select Environment.

3. Deselect the Show QuickTips box.

4. Click OK.

In this lesson, you learned how to use WordPerfect's online Help and how to use the PerfectExpert to answer questions and guide you through tasks. In the next lesson, you will learn how to create a new document.

4

CREATING A NEW DOCUMENT

In this lesson, you'll learn how to create a new document (from scratch or with a template) and how to enter text, move around in a document, and change document views.

CREATING A DOCUMENT FROM SCRATCH

Whenever you start WordPerfect, a blank page appears so that you can immediately begin typing. Think of it as a piece of paper rolled into a typewriter for you! You can open a new blank document like this one at any time when you're working in WordPerfect.

To start a new blank document, click the New Blank Document button on the WordPerfect Toolbar. WordPerfect displays a blank page that's identical to the screen you see when you select the Create a new document option from the Welcome screen. Notice that the title bar at the top of the screen now shows that you are in "Document2."

If you had already typed text into Document1 before you clicked the New Blank Document button, don't panic. That text is still there—the new document is just on top of it. To switch between open document windows, open the Window menu and select the name of the document you want. You'll learn more about working with multiple document windows in Lesson 10.

STARTING A NEW DOCUMENT WITH A TEMPLATE

If you need to create a document that uses a standard format, such as a memo, you can use a *template*. Using templates to create your documents saves you time because the formatting options (the fonts, margins, line spacing, and so on) are automatically set up. All you have to do is type the text and, if necessary, make a few simple changes to the format to fit your needs.

 Template   A ready-made form for a particular document type, such as a letter, memo, or calendar. A template can include both formatting settings (such as margins and headings) and standard text (such as the closing to a sales letter). Every document—even the blank one that appears when you start the program—is based on a template.

WordPerfect provides many *templates* that you can use. Follow these steps to start a new document from a template:

1. Open the File menu and select New. The Select New Document dialog box appears (see Figure 4.1).

First select a document type...   ...and then select a template.

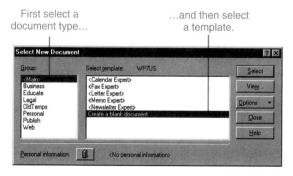

FIGURE 4.1   The Select New Document dialog box.

2. From the Group list on the left, select the type of template you want.

3. Choose a template from the Select template list.

4. (Optional) If you want to look at a template before you open it, click View. A Previewer window opens to display the template.

5. Click Select, and WordPerfect opens a new document based on the template you chose.

 How Do I Close the Previewer Window? When you click Select to select the template (step 5), the Previewer window automatically closes.

6. Depending on which template you select, you may need to fill in information about the document you're creating (see Figure 4.2). Tab to each field and type the requested information. Click OK when you're done.

Click here to change the style.

Advance from one field to the next by pressing the Tab key.

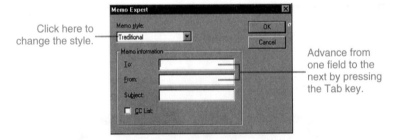

FIGURE 4.2 Fill in information about your document.

 So Many Choices Many templates have more than one predefined style from which you can choose. For example, the memo template has four styles: Traditional, Cosmopolitan, Elegant, and Contemporary. As shown in Figure 4.2, you can choose a style from the drop-down list.

USING PERSONAL INFORMATION

You can add personal information such as your name and company when you use a template that requires it. Once you've added your personal information, WordPerfect stores it for use in future templates. Follow these steps to add personal information the first time you choose a template that requires it:

1. Create a document using a template as described earlier in this lesson. For example, create a document using the Expense report template from the Business Group.

2. In the Template Information dialog box, click Personal Information. The Address Book-Personal Information dialog box appears.

3. Choose Add, and the Properties for New Entry dialog box appears. Follow the system prompts to enter your personal information. (This dialog box looks just like a regular Address Book entry.)

 TIP **That's Me** You'll need to enter your personal information only once. After that, WordPerfect remembers it and enters it in templates as necessary.

4. When you have completed all of the necessary personal information, WordPerfect adds your entry to the My Addresses tab of the Address Book.

5. Highlight your entry and click Select to enter your personal information in both the Address Book and the Expense Report template. WordPerfect also stores the information so it can use the information in other templates that require it.

To change your personal information at any time, follow these steps:

1. Click the Address Book button on the Toolbar to open the Address Book.

2. On the My Addresses tab, highlight your entry and click Edit.

3. Make the necessary changes in the Properties dialog box, and then click OK to return to the My Addresses tab.

4. Click Close to return to the document screen and register your changes. The new information appears the next time you select a template that uses personal information.

Entering Text

As soon as WordPerfect opens to a blank page, you can begin typing. The blinking vertical line, called the *cursor,* shows you where the next character you type will appear. To insert new text, simply move the cursor to the place where you want to begin, and then start typing. You'll learn how to move the cursor around in the next section.

Cursor The blinking vertical line on the screen that indicates where text or codes will be inserted or deleted. The cursor is sometimes called the *insertion point.*

Shadow Pointer As you move the mouse through your document, a thin gray line called a shadow pointer moves through the text. This pointer shows exactly where the cursor will be when you click the mouse.

As you type, keep the following tips in mind:

- When you're typing text and you get to the end of a line, you don't have to press the Enter key. WordPerfect's *word-wrap* feature moves the text from the end of one line to the beginning of the next as you type.

- Press Enter only when you want to end a paragraph or a short line such as a heading or title. Press Enter twice after a paragraph to insert a blank line between that paragraph and the next one.

- Press the Tab key at the beginning of a paragraph to indent the first line of the paragraph to the first tab stop. (You can do the same thing with WordPerfect's Indent feature; you'll learn about using tabs and indents in Lesson 14.)

- You cannot use the down arrow key to move down past the last text in a document. To move below the last word, you must press Enter. (Remember, however, that each time you press Enter, WordPerfect inserts a new blank line.)

- You may not always be able to see all of the text you've typed on-screen. Because your computer screen displays text differently than it would appear on a piece of paper, parts of the text may disappear from view after you type several lines. Later in this lesson, you will learn how to bring that text back into view using the scroll bars.

MOVING AROUND IN A DOCUMENT

Once you have typed some text, you can start moving the cursor around in the document. You can move the cursor using either the keyboard or the mouse, as explained in the following sections.

USING THE KEYBOARD

Using the keyboard is sometimes the easiest way to move around in a document. To move around with the keyboard, use the keys and key combinations listed in Table 4.1.

TABLE 4.1   CURSOR MOVEMENT KEYS

PRESS	TO MOVE
↑	Up one line
↓	Down one line
←	One character to the left
→	One character to the right
Ctrl+↑	Up one paragraph
Ctrl+↓	Down one paragraph
Ctrl+←	One word to the left
Ctrl+→	One word to the right
End	To the end of the current line
Home	To the beginning of the current line
PgUp	To the top of the current screen
PgDn	To the bottom of the current screen
Alt+PgUp	To the first line of the previous page
Alt+PgDn	To the first line of the next page
Ctrl+Home	To the beginning of the document
Ctrl+End	To the end of the document

USING THE MOUSE AND SCROLL BARS

Using the mouse to move around in the visible part of your document is simple: you just click in the place you want the cursor to be. But what if you want to go to a section of text that you can't see anymore, such as the first paragraph of a three-page document? Well, that's when you use the *scroll bars*.

The scroll bars along the right side and the bottom of the screen (see Figure 4.3) enable you to move rapidly through your document. By clicking in the horizontal scroll bar, you can scroll text from left to right across the screen. By clicking on the vertical scroll bar, you can view text that has scrolled off the top or the bottom of the screen.

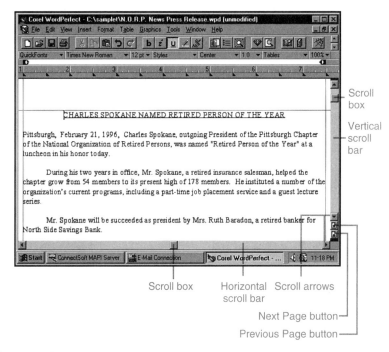

Figure 4.3   Using the mouse, you can move through a document quickly with the scroll bars, arrows, and buttons.

You can use the following techniques to move around your document using the scroll bars:

- Click a scroll arrow at the end of the scroll bar to scroll up, down, right, or left one line or character at a time. To scroll continuously in the direction of the arrow, hold down the mouse button.

- Drag the scroll box within the scroll bar to move to a relative position in your document. For example, you can drag the scroll box to the middle of the vertical scroll bar to move to the middle of the document.

- Click in the gray area of the scroll bar, between the scroll arrow and scroll box, to move one screen forward or backward (using the vertical scroll bar) or left or right (using the horizontal scroll bar).

- Click the Previous Page or the Next Page button on the vertical scroll bar to move a page at a time through the document.

As you scroll, you see different areas of the document on-screen. You should note, however, that scrolling does not change the cursor position. Suppose, for example, that you want to scroll up two pages and add a word. After you scroll to the correct area of the screen, you have to click somewhere in the visible area of the document to move the cursor there. (If you start to type the word without moving the cursor, you immediately find yourself back at the actual cursor position, which is where WordPerfect inserts the text.)

CHANGING THE SCREEN VIEW

WordPerfect for Windows 95 has a *WYSIWYG* screen. Therefore, you don't have to preview your document before you print it. However, you can change how WordPerfect displays the text by choosing from three modes:

- **Draft mode** shows only the text of the document, without showing margins, headers or footers, or page numbers.

- **Page mode** displays the document as if the work area were a blank sheet of paper. For example, if you set a one-inch top margin, the text appears approximately one inch from the top of the work area.

- **Two Page mode** shows two pages of the document at the same time. It's difficult to read the text when you use this mode, but you can see the full layout of each of the pages.

To switch between modes, open the View menu and select Draft, Page, or Two Page. You can change your screen view as often as you like.

 WYSIWYG   WYSIWYG (pronounced Wizzeewig) stands for What You See Is What You Get and means that what you see on the screen is a very close approximation of how your page will look when it is printed. Both Page mode and Two Page mode show your document in WYSIWYG.

In this lesson, you learned how to create a blank document, how to type text, and how to move around a document. You also learned how to change your page view. In the next lesson, you'll learn how to edit text.

EDITING TEXT

In this lesson, you'll learn how to add text, type over existing text, and correct typing errors.

INSERTING TEXT

You can insert text anywhere in a WordPerfect document. For example, you may want to insert a sentence in the middle of a paragraph or add a word to the beginning of an existing sentence. To add text, perform the following steps:

1. Move the cursor to the place where you want to add the text.

2. Type the text. As you type, WordPerfect moves the existing text to the right and adjusts, or wraps, the rest of the text.

Lost Your Cursor? If you use the scroll bars or the Previous Page or Next Page buttons to move through your document, you must click within the document to position the cursor before you start typing. (If you don't, you'll find yourself and your new text back at the old cursor location.)

TYPING OVER EXISTING TEXT

When you start WordPerfect, you are in *Insert* mode. This means that as you type, new text appears to the left of the cursor, and the existing text automatically moves to the right and downward.

However, sometimes you don't want to push the existing text out of the way—you want to type over it. To use *Typeover* mode, in which the new text replaces the existing text, follow these steps:

1. Position the cursor at the beginning of the text you want to replace.

2. Press the Insert key to switch from Insert mode to Typeover mode. (The word **Typeover** appears on the left side of the Status Bar at the bottom of the screen.)

3. Start typing. Each character that you type replaces an existing character.

4. When you finish typing over the existing text, press the Insert key again to switch back to Insert mode. (The word **Insert** reappears on the Status Bar.)

 A Quick Mode Change You can double-click the word Insert on the Status Bar to switch to Typeover mode. When you finish using Typeover mode, double-click the word Typeover to return to Insert mode.

CORRECTING THAT OOPS!

It's easy to make the minor corrections you need to fix typing mistakes or to delete extra words or sentences in your document. To delete characters or words from your document, use any of the following techniques:

- Place the cursor to the left of the character you want to delete and press Delete.

- Place the cursor to the right of the character you want to delete and press Backspace.

- To delete a whole word, double-click the word to select it and press Delete.

- To delete a sentence, triple-click anywhere in the sentence to select it and press Delete.

- To delete an entire paragraph, quadruple-click anywhere in the paragraph to select it and press Delete. Alternatively, you can move the mouse pointer around in the left margin until the pointer changes to a right-pointing arrow. Then double-click to select the paragraph and press Delete.

 The Big Jobs In Lesson 6, you'll learn how to delete, copy, and move blocks of text to make major changes to your documents.

CORRECTING MISTAKES WITH QUICKCORRECT

QuickCorrect is one of your very best friends in WordPerfect! As you type, the QuickCorrect feature automatically fixes such common typos as "oyu" for "you" and "teh" for "the." QuickCorrect is turned on by default, so it goes to work for you as soon as you start WordPerfect.

You can even customize QuickCorrect to automatically fix words that you often misspell. Follow these steps to add words to QuickCorrect's list of misspelled words:

1. Open the Tools menu and select QuickCorrect. The QuickCorrect dialog box appears, as shown in Figure 5.1.

2. In the Replace text box, type the word the way you normally misspell it (such as **leafs**).

3. In the With text box, type the correct spelling for that word (such as **leaves**).

4. Click Add Entry.

5. Check the Replace words as you type check box if it doesn't already contain a check mark.

6. Click Close to return to your document.

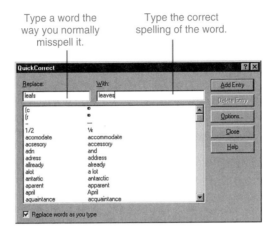

FIGURE 5.1 Add an entry to QuickCorrect

QuickCorrect also corrects other errors, such as two uppercase letters at the beginning of a word or sentence, and double-spacing between sentences. Additionally, QuickCorrect has Format-As-You-Go options that sense what type of text you're typing and format it for you as you type.

For example, if you press the Caps Lock key accidentally and type "dOGS," QuickCorrect will change the word to "Dogs" and turn off Caps Lock for you as you continue to type your document. You can change any of the QuickCorrect options. To do so, click the Options button in the QuickCorrect dialog box, and then select or deselect the options to turn them on or off according to your needs.

It Didn't Work!   QuickCorrect can fix only the words on
the QuickCorrect list. So if, for example, you tell it to replace the misspelling "tixt" with "text" and you accidentally type "ttex" in your document, QuickCorrect will not
correct the mistake. (Of course, if you run the Spell
Checker, that program will find it. You'll learn about the
Spell Checker in Lesson 23.)

Anytime you want to turn off QuickCorrect, select Tools and
choose QuickCorrect. Click the Replace words as you type check
box to remove the check mark, and then click Close to return to
your document.

UNDOING YOUR CHANGES

As you make editing changes to your document, WordPerfect
stores them in a temporary buffer. As a result, you can reverse
your last editing change with the Undo command. For example,
if you accidentally delete a word, or if you move a sentence and
then decide you don't like its new position, you can undo the
error. However, you must use the Undo command *immediately*
after you make the mistake. Once you make another change to
your document, you cannot use the Undo command to fix the
previous change. (However, you can undo the change using another method; see the steps below.)

 To undo your last editing change, open the Edit menu and
select Undo, or click the Undo button on the Toolbar.

 Undo Redo   You can undo your last Undo command by
selecting the Edit, Redo command or by clicking the
Redo button on the Toolbar (the curving arrow that points
to the right).

By default, the Undo feature stores the ten most recent changes you've made to a document. You can increase this number if you want to. The important thing to remember, though, is that you can undo only the one most recent change with the Undo command or Toolbar button.

To restore older changes, perform the following steps:

1. Open the Edit menu and select Undo/Redo History. The Undo/Redo History dialog box appears, as shown in Figure 5.2.

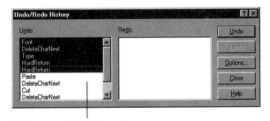

All changes listed above the one you select will also be undone.

FIGURE 5.2 You can reverse older editing changes using the Undo/Redo History command.

2. Changes appear in chronological order, with the most recent one at the top. Select the last editing change you want to undo. (When you choose any item other than the top item, all the items from the selected item to the top of the list are also selected.)

3. Click Undo, and the changes you undo are transferred to the Redo column.

4. Click Close to close the Undo/Redo History dialog box and return to the document screen.

Play It Safe! To increase the number of editing changes WordPerfect stores in its buffer, click the Options button in the Undo/Redo History dialog box. Type a number (say, 50) and click OK.

In this lesson, you learned how to insert text, type over existing text, correct small typing errors, and undo your editing actions. In the next lesson, you will learn how to select blocks of text and make changes to them.

WORKING WITH BLOCKS OF TEXT

In this lesson, you'll learn how to select, move, copy, and delete text blocks.

SELECTING TEXT BLOCKS

A text block consists of any amount of text that you select to perform an action on. You might want to make any number of editing changes in your document. For example, you might want to move a sentence or paragraph from one place to another, or you might want to underline several words in a sentence to add emphasis. Before you can make any of these types of changes however, you must *select* (highlight) the text to tell WordPerfect which text you want to work with. Then you perform the desired command.

Follow these steps to select text with the mouse:

1. Place the mouse pointer on the first letter of the text you want to select.

2. Press the mouse button and drag the mouse until you reach the end of the section of text you want to work with.

3. Release the mouse button, and the block becomes highlighted, as shown in Figure 6.1.

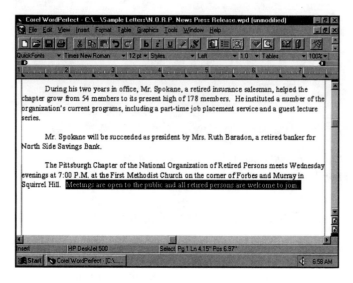

During his two years in office, Mr. Spokane, a retired insurance salesman, helped the chapter grow from 54 members to its present high of 178 members. He instituted a number of the organization's current programs, including a part-time job placement service and a guest lecture series.

Mr. Spokane will be succeeded as president by Mrs. Ruth Baradon, a retired banker for North Side Savings Bank.

The Pittsburgh Chapter of the National Organization of Retired Persons meets Wednesday evenings at 7:00 P.M. at the First Methodist Church on the corner of Forbes and Murray in Squirrel Hill. Meetings are open to the public and all retired persons are welcome to join.

FIGURE 6.1 A selected block of text.

Keyboard Select To select text using the keyboard, move the cursor to the beginning of the block you want to highlight. Hold down the Shift key and move the cursor to the end of the text block. Release the Shift key, and the text becomes selected.

To deselect selected text, click anywhere in the document or press one of the arrow keys.

Character by Character As you select text, you'll notice that WordPerfect automatically selects text one character at a time. If you'd rather select text one word at a time, select Edit, Preferences, double-click the Environment icon, and select Automatically select words. Click OK, and then click Close.

You can quickly select larger blocks of text such as sentences, paragraphs, whole pages, or even the entire document by following these steps:

1. Click the mouse pointer anywhere within the sentence, paragraph, or page you want to select.

2. Open the Edit menu and choose Select. The Select submenu shown in Figure 6.2 appears.

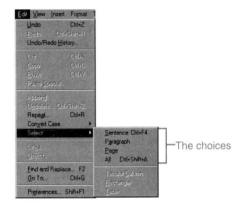

FIGURE 6.2   Choose the option for the amount of text you want to select.

3. Select Sentence, Paragraph, Page, or All. The sentence, paragraph, page, or document in which the cursor is located becomes highlighted. If the cursor is located in a column, a rectangular block, or a table, those options are also available on the submenu. Select one of them to have WordPerfect highlight that section of text.

TIP

Right-Click to Select   To quickly select text, right-click in the margin to the left of the text. In the shortcut menu that appears, click the item you want to select (Sentence, Paragraph, Page, or All).

DELETING A TEXT BLOCK

In Lesson 5, you learned how to delete small portions of text with the Delete and Backspace keys. Although you can do that for larger sections of text, deleting a paragraph or a page one letter at a time can take a long time. To delete a section of text more quickly, select the text block and press the Delete or Backspace key to delete the selected block.

If you want to delete a section of text and replace it with new text, WordPerfect has a shortcut method. You can delete the block of text and replace it with new text in one simple step. Simply select the text you want to delete and then type the new text. The new text you type replaces the old text in your document.

> **Undoing a Deletion** If you accidentally delete text, immediately click the Undo button on the Toolbar to restore it.
>
> **TIP**

COPYING AND MOVING TEXT BLOCKS

To copy or move text, you use one of two command combinations: Copy and Paste or Cut and Paste. You can choose these commands from the Edit menu, or you can use the buttons on the WordPerfect Toolbar.

Copy makes a mirror image of the selected text and places the image on the Clipboard, leaving the original text block intact in your document.

Cut removes the selected block of text from the document (as if you cut it out with a pair of scissors) and places it on the Clipboard.

Paste places the contents of the Clipboard at the cursor location, which might be in the current document, in another WordPerfect document, or even in a document in another Windows-based application.

When you copy or cut a selected block of text, it is sent to a temporary storage location called the Windows *Clipboard*.

Clipboard The Clipboard is a common holding area used by all Windows-based programs. When you copy or cut an item in a document, that data is sent to the Clipboard for temporary storage, where it remains until the next time you copy or cut data or until you end your Windows session.

Text remains on the Clipboard even after you paste it, so you can paste a selection as many times as you need to. If you want to repeat the phrase "Fourth of July" several times in a letter, for example, you can simply type it once, select the phrase, and click the Copy button to copy it to the Clipboard. Then all you have to do is click the Paste button to place it in your document as many times as you want.

If you want to copy or move a text block to the Clipboard without replacing the text that's already there, select the new block in your document, open the Edit menu, and select Append. WordPerfect tacks the new block onto the end of the Clipboard's current contents.

Proceed with Care! Once you copy or cut a new block of text to the Clipboard, the text that was already there is wiped off. Even clicking the Undo button won't bring text back to the Clipboard.

The steps to copy and move text are very similar, but there are two distinct differences in the operations:

- When you *copy* text, the original text remains exactly where it is, and WordPerfect places a copy of the text on the Clipboard so you can paste it wherever you want.

- When you *move* text, WordPerfect removes it from the document and places it on the Clipboard. From there, you can paste it into one or more new locations.

 Moving and Cutting The terms "moving" and "cutting" mean essentially the same thing: you remove text from its current position and relocate it in another.

There are a couple of ways to copy or move text to a new location. If you can see the new location on the screen, *drag and drop* the text by following these steps:

1. Select the text block you want to move or copy.

2. To *move* text, position the mouse pointer over the selected text, and then press and hold down the left mouse button. A small rectangle appears.

   To *copy* text, press and hold the Ctrl key, position the mouse pointer over the selected text, and then press and hold the left mouse button. A small rectangle with a plus sign inside appears.

3. Drag the mouse pointer (which is followed by the rectangle or the rectangle with the plus sign) to the desired location. Release the mouse button (and then the Ctrl key if necessary). WordPerfect moves or copies the text to the new position.

If you can't see the new location for the text on the screen, use the following steps to copy or move text. (This method works best when you want to copy text to another document in WordPerfect or to a document in another program.)

1. Select the text block you want to copy or move.

2. Click the Copy or Cut button on the Toolbar.

3. Move the cursor to the position in the document where you want the text to appear. (You can switch to another document or Windows program if necessary.)

4. Click the Paste button on the Toolbar. The copied or moved text appears in the new location.

The Button's Not Available! The Copy and Cut buttons become "active" only after you select text.

TIP **Pretty Smart, Eh?** When you paste text from the Clipboard, WordPerfect adds or deletes spaces at the new location as necessary.

In this lesson, you learned how to select, delete, copy, and move text blocks. In the next lesson, you will learn how to save and close your documents.

SAVING AND CLOSING DOCUMENTS

In this lesson, you'll learn how to save the document you're working on and how to close the document to remove it from the screen.

SAVING A DOCUMENT

When you open a document and start typing, the document that you see on-screen exists only in the temporary memory of your computer. If you exit WordPerfect without saving your document, or if the electricity is turned off, your document is lost. In order to keep a permanent record of your work, you must name the document and save it to a folder on your computer's hard disk or to a floppy disk.

SAVING A DOCUMENT FOR THE FIRST TIME

The first time you save a document, you must assign a file name and tell WordPerfect which folder to store the file in.

 File   A collection of information (your document) stored as a single unit on a floppy disk or on your computer's hard disk. Every file has a file name that's used to identify it.

Follow these steps to save your document for the first time:

 1. Open the File menu and choose Save, or click the Save button on the Toolbar. The Corel Office—Save As dialog box appears (see Figure 7.1).

2. From the Save in list, select a drive and folder to save the document in. If you want, you can use the WordPerfect default, which saves your document in the C:\MyFiles folder.

3. Type a name for your document in the Name text box. The name can be up to 256 characters and can contain punctuation and spaces. If you don't specify a file extension (the three-character code after the period at the end of the file name), WordPerfect automatically adds a .WPD extension.

4. (Optional) Click the Password Protect check box to add a password to the file.

5. When you have entered all the information, click Save.

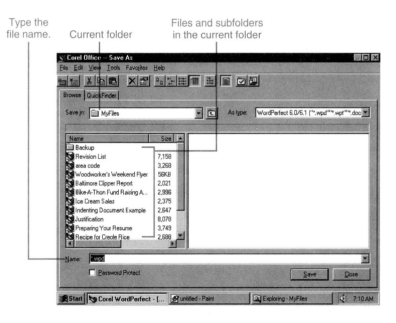

FIGURE 7.1   The first time you save a file, the Corel Office—Save As dialog box appears.

Saving Your Document Again

After you save your document for the first time, you can continue working on it. As with text you type in a blank document, the changes you make to an existing document are stored in temporary memory; they are not permanent until you save the file again. Therefore, you must remember to save your document on a regular basis. If you get into a routine of saving your document at regular intervals, say every 15 minutes or so, you aren't likely to lose important changes that you make to the file.

Saving a document again is a piece of cake. Open the File menu and choose Save, or click the Save button on the Toolbar. WordPerfect records the changes you've made since the last time you saved the document.

Using the Save As Command

The Save As command is similar to the Save command. But instead of overwriting the old file name with the new changes as you do with Save, you can use Save As to do these things:

- Save the file with a different name

- Change the drive and folder in which the file is stored

- Save the file in a different file *format*

For example, suppose you open a file (see Lesson 8) named "Draft of Sales Agreement-Version 1." You can make some changes and then save the document using the name "Draft of Sales Agreement-Version 2." The Version 1 document remains intact, and you've got a new document that you didn't have to create from scratch.

When you use the Save command to save a file, WordPerfect saves it in WordPerfect 7 format. However, you can save files in a number of other file formats, including prior versions of WordPerfect. If you are planning to give the file to someone who is not using WordPerfect for Windows 95, you need to save the file in a format that he can open on his computer.

TIP **Previous Version** Whenever you use Save As to save a file, WordPerfect defaults to the WordPerfect 6.0/6.1 format. You can use Save As to save your WordPerfect 7 document in 6.0/6.1 format, giving it a different file name than you did originally.

To save an existing file with a different name or file format, follow these steps:

1. Open the File menu and choose Save As. The Corel Office—Save As dialog box appears, with the file name shown in the Name text box and WordPerfect 6.0/6.1 as the file format in the As type text box.

2. To change the name, format, or location options of the file, do the following:

   - To save the file with a different name, type the new name in the Name text box. (Because the file name is already highlighted, the existing name disappears as soon as you start typing.)

   - To save the file to another location, you can type the complete path (such as C:\Desktop\Vacation Plans\Hawaii Intinerary.wpd) in the Name box. If you're not sure of the exact path, click the Save in drop-down arrow to open My Computer and browse through the folders to find the folder you want. (You might need to use the scroll bars to find it.) When you find the folder, click its name to open it.

   - To save the file with a different file format, open the As type drop-down list and select the desired file format.

3. When you have entered all of the necessary information, click Save to save the file and return to the document screen.

Password Protection Warning   If you want to assign a password to a file to make it more secure, click the Password Protect check box. You'll be prompted to type and then verify the password. Be very careful using this option. If you forget the password, WordPerfect won't let you open the file again.

CLOSING A FILE

When you finish creating or editing a document, you can close it. Then you can continue working with other WordPerfect documents, or you can exit the program (see Lesson 1). WordPerfect allows you to have up to nine documents open at a time. If you close all nine, WordPerfect opens a new Document1 window for you to work in.

To close a document, open the File menu and choose Close. If you have made changes to the document since the last time you saved it, you will be asked if you want to save it. If you have not modified it since the last save, WordPerfect closes the document window.

In this lesson, you learned how to save and close your documents. In the next lesson, you'll learn how to print in WordPerfect, open existing WordPerfect documents, and open files created using other applications. You'll also learn how to work with multiple document windows.

RETRIEVING DOCUMENTS

In this lesson, you'll learn how to open existing WordPerfect documents and files created using other applications. You'll also learn how to work with multiple document windows.

OPENING EXISTING DOCUMENTS

As you learned in Lesson 7, when you save a document, you create a *file* that Windows 95 stores in a folder on disk. This file contains all of the information needed to recreate the file on the screen when you open it again.

Follow these steps to open a document file from within WordPerfect:

1. Click the Open button on the Toolbar, or open the File menu and click Open. The Corel Office—Open dialog box appears, as shown in Figure 8.1.

> **TIP** **Memories, Memories** If the file you want to open is one of the last nine you've opened previously, you can open the File menu and select the name of the file from the list at the bottom of the menu. WordPerfect remembers the names and locations of the last nine files you opened.

2. In the Corel Office—Open dialog box, locate and open the file you want using one of these methods:

- If the file you want to open is in the current default folder (MyFiles), click the file name once to select it and click the Open button. (You might need to use the scroll bars to find the file you want.)

Select a document
from the list.

A preview of the
selected file

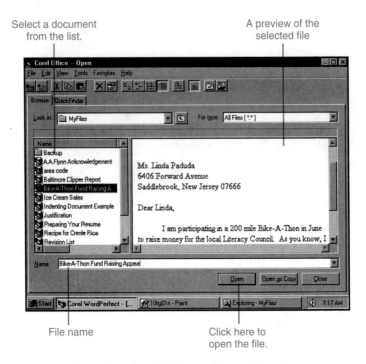

File name

Click here to
open the file.

FIGURE 8.1   The Corel Office—Open dialog box.

- If the file you want to open is in a different folder or on a floppy disk, you can type the complete path (such as C:\Desktop\Budget Reports\Third Quarter.wpd) in the Name box.

- Click the Look in drop-down arrow to open My Computer and browse through the folders to find the file (see Figure 8.2). When you find the file, click it.

3. Click Open. WordPerfect opens a new document window and displays your file.

FIGURE 8.2 Browse through the folders on your computer or a floppy disk to find the file you want.

What a View Want to see what's in a file before you open it? While you're in the Open dialog box, select View point to Preview, and select Content, Page View, or Use separate window. Or, click the View button on the Corel Office—Open Toolbar. Select a file from the file list box, and WordPerfect displays a preview of the file on the preview screen.

Windows Explorer Buttons Many of the buttons on the Toolbar in the Corel Office—Open dialog box are similar to buttons found in Windows Explorer. You can use the Open dialog box in place of Explorer for many file management tasks, including copying and moving files, creating new folders, and so on.

OPENING FILES USING FAVORITES

If you frequently store files to other drives or folders, you might want to add items to your list of Favorites. Choosing an item from the Favorites list is a shortcut for locating and then opening the folder or file on your computer.

When you create a shortcut using Favorites, the shortcut is stored in a folder called Favorites on your hard drive. (The actual folders or files themselves remain in their original locations.) The shortcuts stored in the Favorites folder enable WordPerfect to go quickly to those locations so that you don't need to move to them when you want to open a favorite file or folder. To add a file or folder to the Favorites list, follow these steps:

1. Click the Open Toolbar button or select the File, Open command to access the Open dialog box.

2. Open the folder you want to add to the Favorites folder. If you want to add a file, select the file's name.

3. Open the Favorites menu, select Add, and click Add to Favorites. WordPerfect immediately adds a shortcut to the Favorites folder.

The next time you want to open a file or open a file stored in a folder you have added to the Favorites folder, open the Favorites drop-down list and click the folder name.

Opening Files Created with Other Programs

WordPerfect contains tools for opening files created with other programs. WordPerfect allows you to open files created in approximately 50 other programs. In addition, WordPerfect imports data created in spreadsheet and database programs.

Document conversion is easy. If you want to open a file that was created by another program, open it just as you would any WordPerfect file (which you learned to do earlier in this lesson). The conversion process begins, opening a Convert File Format dialog box. As WordPerfect converts the file, you'll see a Conversion in Progress box. When the conversion is complete, the document appears on-screen, ready for you to edit.

 Conversion Woes The results of a file conversion are not always perfect because some formatting codes do not translate completely. Check the converted file carefully.

FINDING A FILE USING QUICKFINDER

QuickFinder helps you find a saved document whose name or location you don't remember. QuickFinder can search through multiple folders and drives to locate the misplaced file. These steps teach you how to use QuickFinder.

1. Click the Open Toolbar button or select the File, Open command to access the Open dialog box.

2. Click the QuickFinder tab to see the options displayed in Figure 8.3.

Fast Search Setup   The first time you use QuickFinder, the QuickFinder Fast Search Setup Expert dialog box appears. Click the **PreSearch** button to have WordPerfect periodically presearch the files stored in your computer while you work. Then, when you use QuickFinder, the search for the file you're looking for will be faster.

3. Enter whatever information you know about the file, using one of these methods:

- If you know the name of the file, or at least a portion of the name, type it in the Name text box using *wild cards* as needed. For example, if you know the file name began with the words "Baltimore Clipper," enter **Baltimore Clipper*.*** in the box.

- Type some words that you know are in the file (such as "Linda Paduda") in the Content text box. Try to make the text as specific to that file as possible.

Wild Cards   Wild cards are symbols that take the place of characters you don't know. The question mark (?) stands for a single character, and the asterisk (*) stands for multiple characters.

Type a file name or a few
words of file-specific text.

Browse to find
the folder.

Results will be
displayed here.

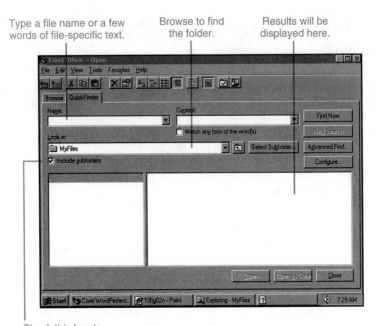

Check this box to
search in subfolders.

FIGURE 8.3   Use QuickFinder to find a file you can't seem to
locate.

4. In the Look in box, select the drive and/or folder you
   want to search.

5. (Optional) To look in all the folder's subfolders, check the
   Include subfolders check box. Or, to look in a particular
   subfolder, click Select Subfolder, choose the subfolder,
   and then click Select.

6. When you finish setting the search criteria, click Find
   Now. WordPerfect searches for the file. All of the file
   names that match the specifications appear in the File
   names box.

7. Select the file you want and click Open.

VIEWING MULTIPLE DOCUMENTS

WordPerfect provides the ability to work with multiple documents. For example, suppose you're creating a new contract and you need to refer to a document that contains information about an old contract. Instead of printing one and then working from that hard copy, you can open both of them on-screen.

You can *cascade* or *tile* multiple documents on the WordPerfect screen. Figures 8.4 and 8.5 show cascaded and tiled document windows, respectively.

Cascade   To arrange all of the open documents so that they are neatly stacked and only the title bars show behind the active window.

Tile   To arrange the open documents so that they can all be seen at once.

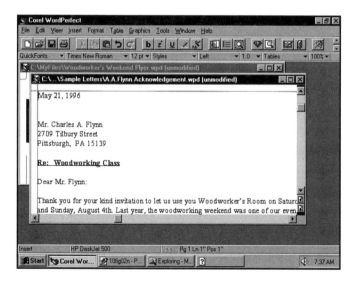

FIGURE 8.4   Cascaded windows overlap so that only the title bars show behind the active window.

FIGURE 8.5   Tiled windows occupy equal amounts of space on the screen.

To cascade or tile document windows follow these steps:

1. Open the documents you want to view.

2. Open the Window menu and choose Cascade, Tile Top to Bottom, or Tile Side by Side. WordPerfect arranges the open windows accordingly.

3. To switch to an open window, simply click its title bar to make it active.

To maximize an open window (make it fill the screen), click its Maximize button. To switch to another open document window that you can't see, open the Window menu and click the name of the document you want to go to. (Remember that a document must be open for its name to appear on the Window list.)

In this lesson, you learned to open files and work with multiple documents on the screen. In the next lesson, you'll learn how to print your document.

PRINTING YOUR DOCUMENT

9

In this lesson, you'll learn how to print your document.

GETTING READY TO PRINT

You can print your document whenever you like. When you send a job to your printer, Windows 95 must communicate to your printer in the printer's own language, which it does by means of a *printer driver*. Because WordPerfect uses the printer and driver that you installed in Windows 95, you should not have to do anything else to set up the printer for use with WordPerfect. (If you need help installing a printer in Windows 95, refer to your Windows 95 documentation.)

 Driver   A program that provides Windows with the information it needs to work with a specific device such as a printer.

If the correct printer is not selected however, the printer driver WordPerfect uses will not work correctly and the printed document might not look at all like your document. Therefore, if you're one of the many Windows 95 users who has additional printer drivers installed (such as Microsoft Fax, WinFax, or the Envoy printer driver that can be installed with the WordPerfect 7 suite), you have to pay attention to which printer driver is selected. WordPerfect remembers the last printer to which it sent a job, and if it's not the default printer or printer driver, the name of that device appears on the Status Bar (see Figure 9.1).

The currently selected printer

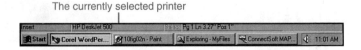

FIGURE 9.1   Check the printer name in the Status Bar.

If the printer name is not correct, or if you want to print to a printer other than the one shown, you must select another printer. Follow these steps to select a different printer:

1. Open the File menu and choose Print, or click the Print button on the Toolbar. The Print dialog box appears.

2. Click the Printer tab to display the settings for the currently selected printer (shown in Figure 9.2).

Click here to return to   Open this list to select
the Print dialog box.   another printer.

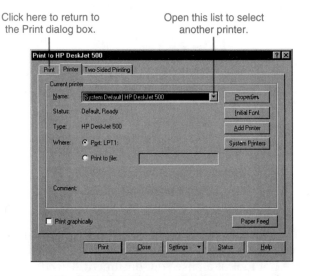

FIGURE 9.2   The Printer options.

    Shortcut to Printer Tab   Double-click the printer name on the Status Bar to access the Printer tab of the Print dialog box.

3. Open the drop-down list and select another installed printer.

4. Click Close to return to your document.

The printer you selected is now the default printer for all documents. You don't need to select a printer for other documents unless you want to print to another printer.

PREVIEWING YOUR DOCUMENT BEFORE YOU PRINT

Before you send your document to print, it's a good idea to preview what the printed pages will look like. Although WordPerfect does not offer a separate print preview command, you can adjust the screen view to see the layout of the pages.

Select View, Page to see how your document will look when it is printed. When you are in Page view, you can zoom out to view the entire page, or you can zoom in to examine your document closely. Follow these steps to change the zoom level:

1. Open the View menu and choose Zoom. The Zoom dialog appears (see Figure 9.3).

FIGURE 9.3 The Zoom dialog box.

2. Select one of the following options or enter a percentage in the Other spin box.

Margin Width displays the text from margin to margin.

Page Width displays the document with blank spaces for margins.

Full Page reduces the document so you can see the entire page.

 Zooming In   Change the zoom quickly by clicking the Zoom button on the Power Bar and then selecting a zoom option from the list that appears.

3. Click OK. WordPerfect displays the document with the selected zoom setting.

 4. Toggle between the current view and Page View/Full Page Zoom by clicking the Page/Zoom Full button on the Toolbar.

 Take Two   Select View, Two Page view to see how two pages look side by side.

PRINTING YOUR DOCUMENT

Once you've made sure that the correct printer is selected and you've previewed your document (and fixed any errors), you're ready to print. The following steps walk you through the process.

 1. Open the File menu and choose Print or click the Print button on the Toolbar. The Print dialog box appears, as shown in Figure 9.4.

Check this box to print graphics.

Open this list to select which pages to print.

Set the number of copies.

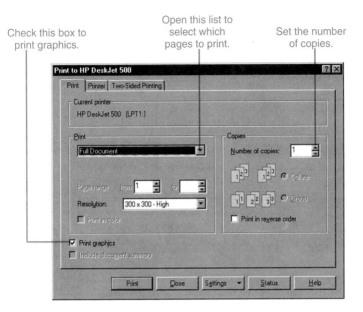

FIGURE 9.4   The Print dialog box.

2. Select which pages to print by opening the Print drop-down list and choosing one of the following options:

Full Document prints all pages of the document.

Current Page prints only the page in which the cursor is located.

Multiple Pages allows you to specify a range of pages (to print pages 3 through 6, for example).

Document on Disk prints the document to a file instead of a printer. (Usually used when no printer is connected to your system.)

Advanced Multiple Pages allows you to print selected pages, such as 1,5,7.

Document on Disk prints the document to a file instead of a printer. (Usually used when no printer is connected to the system.)

3. Type a number in the Number of Copies spin box if you want multiple copies. (You don't need to change this if you want only one copy.)

4. Check Print Graphics if you want clip art and other graphic images to print. (See Lesson 24 for more information about graphics.)

5. When you've set all the desired options, click Print. WordPerfect sends your document to the printer.

Nothing's Coming Out   If your printer doesn't start printing very shortly after you click Print, make sure that the printer is turned on, has paper, and is *online*.(Most printers have a light that shows when the printer is online.)

Back to Front   If your printer feeds the completed pages face up, the last page of your document finishes on top. To reverse that order, choose File, Print. In the Print dialog box, choose Print in reverse order. From now on, your document will print with the first page on top.

USING THE MAKE IT FIT EXPERT

WordPerfect can reformat your document to print on exactly the number of pages you specify. For example, if the last two lines of a letter flow to the second page, you can use Make It Fit to compress the document to one page.

Make It Fit saves you the time-consuming process of manually adjusting the format of the document or the text to fit the desired number of pages. Follow these easy steps to use the Make-It-Fit Expert.

1. Save your document before you begin. If you do that and the results are unsatisfactory, you can close the document and then open it again.

2. Open the Format menu and choose Make It Fit, or click the Make It Fit button on the Toolbar. The Make-It-Fit dialog box appears, as shown in Figure 9.5.

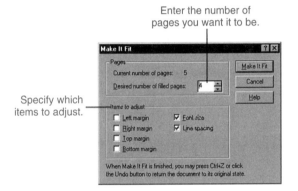

FIGURE 9.5 The Make It Fit dialog box.

3. Indicate the formatting changes you'll allow WordPerfect to make.

4. Click Make It Fit to let WordPerfect reformat your document.

USING BINDING AND TWO-SIDED PRINTING

You can use the binding and two-sided printing options to prepare a document to be bound. These options help you create a document that can be bound on the short edge of the page (like a flip chart) or on the long edge of the page (like a book).

If your printer has two-sided printing capability, you can print your document on both sides of the page by following these steps:

1. Open the File menu and choose Print, or click the Print button on the Toolbar. Click the Two-Sided Printing tab to display two-sided printing options (see Figure 9.6).

Check this box to print your document as a booklet.

Change the offset binding.

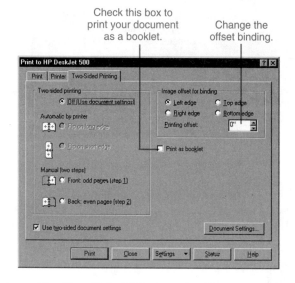

FIGURE 9.6   The Two-Sided Printing tab offers many choices.

2. In the section labeled Automatic by printer, select Flip on long edge to set up the document for binding down the long side or select Flip on short edge to set up the document for binding across the top.

3. Enter a binding offset number in the Printing offset text box.

Binding Offset   The amount of space needed to bind the pages. The number you enter is added to the document margin. For example, if your document margins are all 1" and you need to allow 1.5" on the left side for binding, click the Left edge option button and enter .5" in the Printing offset text box.

4. (Optional) Check Print as booklet if you are planning to print your document in booklet form.

5. When you finish setting the two-sided printing options, click the Print tab if you need to return to the Print dialog box.

6. Click Print to print your document using the two-sided printing options you specified.

If your printer is not capable of two-sided printing, go to the Two-Sided Printing tab and follow these steps:

1. In the section labeled Manual (two steps), select Front: odd pages (step 1) as shown in Figure 9.6 and click Print. WordPerfect prints the odd-numbered pages.

2. Flip the printed pages over and reinsert them in your printer's paper tray or sheet feeder.

3. Select Back: even pages (step 2) and click Print. WordPerfect prints the even pages on the back side of the odd pages.

In this lesson, you learned how to print your document and use some of WordPerfect's advanced printing options. In the next lesson, you'll learn how to create and print envelopes and labels.

10

CREATING ENVELOPES AND LABELS

In this lesson, you'll learn how to create and print envelopes and labels and how to use the Address Book to store addresses.

CREATING ENVELOPES

It's easy to create a matching envelope for any letter. If the on-screen document is in a standard business letter format (in which the mailing address is on the left), WordPerfect can find the address and insert it onto the envelope!

To create an envelope, follow these steps:

1. Open the Format menu and choose Envelope. The Envelope dialog box appears, as shown in Figure 10.1.

Click here to open the Address Book.

Make sure the address is correct.

Check this box to print the return address.

Select the envelope size.

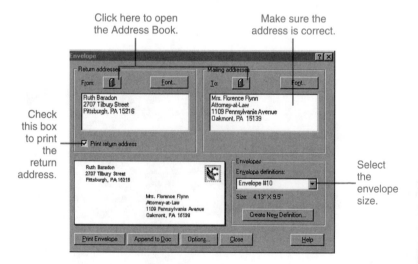

FIGURE 10.1 The Envelope dialog box.

2. Type your return address in the Return addresses box. If the return address is in the Address Book, you can click the Address Book button and double-click the return address you want to add to the envelope. (See Lesson 4 for more about the Address Book.)

3. If the mailing address was not pulled from the on-screen document, type the address in the Mailing addresses box. If the mailing address is in the Address Book, you can click the Address Book button and double-click the entry you want to use as the mailing address.

4. (Optional) If you want to change the typeface for either of the addresses, click the corresponding Font button and select a new font from the list.

5. Select an envelope type from the Envelope definitions drop-down list.

6. If you are ready to print the envelope now, click Print Envelope. If you want to add the envelope text as a separate page at the end of your document, click Append to Doc.

 Two or More   If your document contains more than one mailing address, select the mailing address you want to use on the envelope before you choose Format, Envelope to open the Envelope dialog box.

USING THE ADDRESS BOOK

If you frequently send correspondence to the same people, you can store their names, addresses and other information in WordPerfect's Address Book. Once you have the information in the Address Book, you never need to type it again.

Follow these steps to create an Address Book entry:

1. Click the Address Book button on the Toolbar. The Address Book dialog box appears.

2. Click the My Addresses tab and click Add.

3. From the list in the New Entry dialog box, select either Person or Organization and click OK. The Properties for New Entry dialog box appears.

4. Fill in all applicable fields in the Properties for New Entry dialog box, as shown in Figure 10.2. If you don't want to enter any information in a field, press Tab to move to the next field.

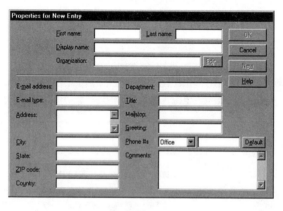

FIGURE 10.2   Complete this form to add an entry to the Address Book.

5. When you finish typing the entry, click OK. You're returned to the Address Book dialog box.

6. (Optional) Click Add to enter additional names.

7. Click Close to close the Address Book and return to the document screen.

Once you have some entries in your Address Book, you can include them in your documents. Follow these steps to use an address from the Address Book on an envelope:

1. Instead of typing the mailing information in the Envelope dialog box, click the Address Book icon under Mailing addresses.

2. Select the name and address entry that you want to use on the envelope.

3. Click OK, and WordPerfect transfers the information to the envelope.

WORKING WITH LABELS

WordPerfect comes with more than 130 predefined label formats for the basic labels available at office supply stores. These include labels for everything from standard address labels and name badges to business cards and video cassettes.

SELECTING A LABEL DEFINITION

Before you create the label, check the name and number of the label style you want to use. For example, if you look at the label package, you'll see a style name such as Avery Address Label, #5160. Follow these simple steps to select a label definition:

1. In a new document, place your cursor at the position where you want the labels to begin.

2. Open the Format menu and choose Labels. The Labels dialog box shown in Figure 10.3 appears.

3. In the Display section, choose Laser if your labels are made on sheets of paper for use with a laser or inkjet-type printer; choose Tractor-fed if your labels are made on sheets with holes along the sides to guide the labels through a dot-matrix printer; or choose Both.

Choose the type of
label to display.

Select your
label from
the list.

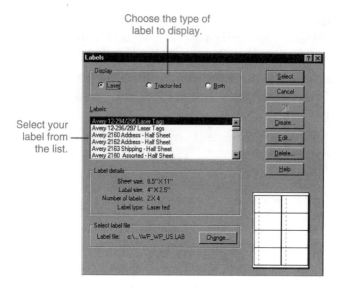

FIGURE 10.3   Fill in the information about your labels.

4. Scroll through the Labels list to find the label you want.
Select it and click Select. WordPerfect displays the label
on-screen, with margin guidelines (see Figure 10.4).

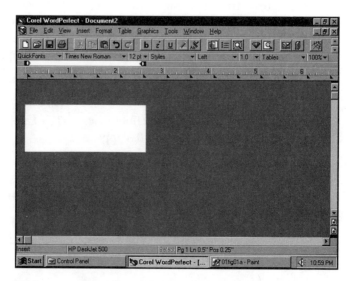

FIGURE 10.4   The first label is shown on the screen.

CREATING A LABEL DEFINITION

Because there are so many predefined labels in WordPerfect, your best bet is to use a label that has already been set up. However, you can create a custom label by following these steps:

1. Open the Format menu and choose Labels. The Labels dialog box appears.

2. Click Create, and the Create Labels dialog box appears.

3. Type a description in the Label description text box.

4. Fill in the boxes for label size and position, labels per page, distance between labels, and label margins.

5. When you have filled in all of the boxes, click OK to return to the Labels dialog box.

6. Click Select to display the label on your screen.

 TIP   **Help Yourself** Before you create a custom label definition, click the definition on the list that most closely matches your label. You can use it as a starting point.

TYPING AND PRINTING LABELS

WordPerfect treats each label like a separate page. To type and then print labels, follow these steps:

1. Type the text normally. If you are typing an address label, press Enter at the end of each line to advance the cursor to the next line.

2. When you complete a label, press Ctrl+Enter to advance to the next label.

3. Insert the blank labels into the printer.

4. Click the Print button on the Toolbar to print the labels.

In this lesson, you learned to create and print envelopes and labels. In the next lesson, you'll learn about hidden codes.

WORKING WITH WORDPERFECT CODES

In this lesson, you'll learn how to view the hidden codes that WordPerfect uses to control your documents and how to delete and edit those codes.

WHAT ARE WORDPERFECT CODES?

Think of WordPerfect codes as commands that format your document. As you type your documents, WordPerfect keeps notes about the formatting options you have selected. For example, when you choose the command to underline, you see the results of the action on-screen (the text becomes underlined). However, you don't see the hidden codes that are placed in your document to tell WordPerfect when to start and stop the underlining. The codes are hidden from your view so that the document screen remains uncluttered.

When WordPerfect encounters a code, say to change the document margins or to add bold text, the program obeys the instructions of the command until it reaches the end of the document or until it finds a new instruction (new code) telling it to change again.

WordPerfect adds these three types of codes to documents:

- **Paired codes**   These codes point at each other to start and stop specific formatting options such as underline or bold. The first code turns on the formatting feature, and the second turns it off. For example, to bold the phrase "This is bold text!," you would select the text and then select the Bold command. WordPerfect then places a hidden code at each end of it. Figure 11.1 shows a set of paired codes. When you insert a paired code into your document, both the code on and code off boxes are inserted with the cursor between them, so you can proceed to enter text.

- **Open codes**   WordPerfect uses open codes for instructions that affect a document from the code forward. For example, if you change the left margin from one to two inches in the middle of the document, WordPerfect inserts the code **[Lft Mar]**, as shown in Figure 11.1. That code affects all of the text that follows it unless you enter another margin change code later on (you might change the left margin back to one inch, for example).

- **Single codes**   WordPerfect uses single codes to show changes that take effect at the position of the cursor. For example, when you press Enter to advance to the next line, WordPerfect places the code **[HRt]** (for hard return) in your document.

Why Should I Care About Codes?   Because codes normally do all of their work in the background, you usually don't have to think about them. However, if your program starts behaving strangely when you're working in a document (for example, if you try to delete a word, and suddenly the screen fills with bold, italic type), you can view the codes to find the cause of the problem and fix it.

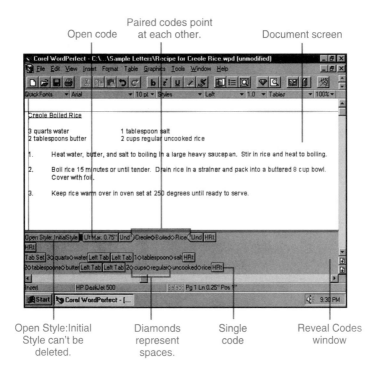

FIGURE 11.1 The Reveal Codes window shows you the codes that control your text.

REVEALING HIDDEN CODES

WordPerfect codes are hidden by default. You can display them using any of the following methods:

- Open the View menu and choose Reveal Codes.

- Right-click in the text and choose Reveal Codes from the QuickMenu that appears.

- Press the Alt+F3 key combination.

When you turn on Reveal Codes, the screen splits into two parts. Normal text appears in the top part of the screen (the document screen), and the text with the codes appears in the lower part (the Reveal Codes window). In the text portion of the screen, you can type, format, and edit your document as you normally would, but now you can also work with the codes.

Normally, with codes showing, 75% of the work area remains available for the document screen (text without codes), and 25% of the screen is given to the Reveal Codes window (text and codes). You can change the proportions of the two screens by following these steps.

1. Place the mouse pointer on the Reveal Codes window's dividing line (the heavy black line between the two parts of the window). The pointer becomes a double-headed arrow, as shown in Figure 11.2.

2. Drag the dividing line upward to make the Reveal Codes screen larger, or drag it downward to make the Document screen larger.

3. Release the mouse button, and WordPerfect adjusts the screen proportions accordingly.

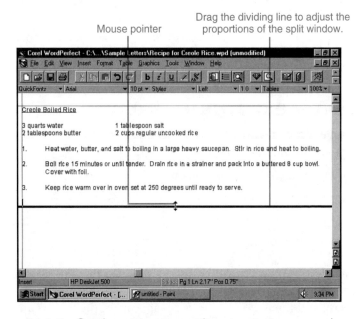

FIGURE 11.2   Set the screen proportions to meet your needs.

To close the Reveal Codes window, press Alt+F3, or select the View, Reveal Codes command, or right-click anywhere in the document window and choose Hide Reveal Codes from the QuickMenu.

REMOVING CODES

When the codes are displayed, you can edit them to change the layout and formatting of your text. You can even delete a code to remove its instruction from your document. For example, if you wanted to remove the bold attribute from the phrase "This is bold text!," you would delete one of the **Bold** paired codes marking the phrase. (If you delete either code in a set of paired codes, the other one is automatically deleted.) Follow these steps to delete a code:

1. If it's not already open, display the Reveal Codes window using one of the methods discussed previously.

2. Click the code you want to delete.

3. Press the Delete key to eliminate the code.

Shortcut! You can also remove a code by dragging it up out of the Reveal Codes window and into the document window.

Oops! If you accidentally delete a code, you can reverse the action by immediately clicking the Undo button on the Toolbar.

CHANGING CODES

If you want to change the formatting set in place by an open code (a code that changes the left margin, for example), follow these steps:

1. In the Reveal Codes window, double-click the code that you want to change. For example, double-click the [Lft Mar] code. The standard dialog box you use to change that option appears.

2. Make your changes as you normally would in the dialog box.

3. Click OK. WordPerfect implements the change from that point forward in the document. The cursor position remains unchanged.

Open Style:Initial Style   Each new document you create begins with an Open Style code that cannot be deleted.

In this lesson, you learned how to display, delete, and edit WordPerfect's hidden codes. In the next lesson, you'll learn how to change the look of your text.

CHANGING THE APPEARANCE OF YOUR TEXT

In this lesson, you'll learn how to change the appearance of your text by changing the font and by adding attributes such as bold, underline, and italics.

CHARACTER FORMATTING

When you type a document, whatever you type appears in plain text. If you want to set off a block of text or emphasize words or phrases, you can change the *formatting* of the plain text. Character formatting affects how text looks. Adding bold, underlining, italics, or different fonts can make important text stand out and give your documents a professional look. Figure 12.1 shows some of the fonts and attributes you have to work with.

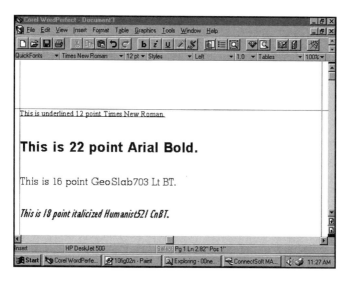

FIGURE 12.1 Examples of several fonts and attributes.

Font Any set of characters with the same typeface and type size. For example, Times New Roman 10-point is a font. Times New Roman is the typeface, and 10-point is the size. (There are 72 points in an inch.)

CHANGING THE FONT SIZE OR ATTRIBUTES OF TEXT

You can change the formatting of existing text, or you can format new text as you type. Here's how to format text as you are typing:

1. Place the cursor where you want the formatting change to take effect.

2. Open the Format menu and select Font. The Font dialog box shown in Figure 12.2 appears.

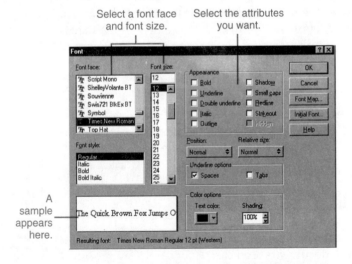

FIGURE 12.2   Select a font and attributes from the Font dialog box.

The Easy Way!   You can also display the Font dialog box by right-clicking anywhere in the document and selecting Font from the QuickMenu.

3. In the Font face and/or Font size list boxes, make a selection. Notice that the sample in the sample box reflects your changes.

4. Choose the attributes you want from the Appearance section of the dialog box.

5. Click OK.

6. Type your text. When you finish typing the text you want to have those attributes, repeat steps 2–5 to turn the attributes off.

Shortcut Keys   Use shortcut keys to make text bold, italic, and underlined. Press Ctrl+B for bold, Ctrl+I for italic, and Ctrl+U for underline. Press the key combination again to turn the attribute off.

Now or Later   To format existing text, select the text first, and then apply the formatting options you want.

CHANGING THE DEFAULT FONT

By default, WordPerfect uses the Times New Roman 12-point font for all new documents. You can change this font for one document or for all new documents by performing the following steps:

1. Open the Format menu and choose Document.

2. Click Initial Font. The Document Initial Font dialog box appears, as shown in Figure 12.3.

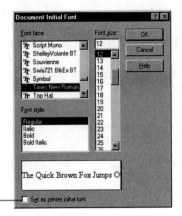

Click here to use this font for all future documents.

FIGURE 12.3 You can change the default font used for all documents.

3. Make your selections from the Font face and/or Font size list boxes.

4. (Optional) To change the default font for this document and future documents you create, click the Set as printer initial font check box.

5. Click OK.

Previously Created Documents If you click the Set as printer initial font check box, the new font affects only the current document and any new documents you create going forward. To change the font in an older document, open the document and change the font as explained earlier in the lesson.

APPLYING ATTRIBUTES USING THE POWER BAR AND THE TOOLBAR

The Toolbar and the Power Bar make it easy to change attributes in your text. Follow these steps to format text using the Toolbar:

1. Position the cursor where you want the attribute to start.

2. Click one of the following Toolbar buttons:

    Bold

   Italic

   Underline

3. Type your text.

4. When you finish typing, turn the attribute off by clicking the button again.

> **For Existing Text**   To change an attribute for existing text, select the text, and then click the appropriate Toolbar button.

The current font and font size always appear on the Power Bar. Click either button to select another font or size. If you need more information about your choice, or if you want to see a sample, double-click the button to open the Font dialog box.

The QuickFonts button on the Power Bar lets you reuse any of the last 10 fonts (including point sizes and attributes) you've most recently selected while using WordPerfect.

Perform these steps to use QuickFonts.

1. Click the QuickFonts button on the Power Bar. A list of the last 10 fonts and attributes you've selected appears, as shown in Figure 12.4.

2. Choose the desired font from the list. New text that you type will appear in the selected font.

FIGURE 12.4   Select a previously used font from the QuickFonts list on the Power Bar.

In this lesson, you learned how to add character formatting to text by changing fonts and adding attributes. In the next lesson, you'll learn to set line spacing and justification.

SETTING THE LINE SPACING AND JUSTIFICATION

In this lesson, you'll learn how to change line spacing and how to align text between the left and right margins.

CHANGING LINE SPACING

The line spacing feature gives you control over the amount of space between the lines of text in your document. You might want to create a document in which the lines are as close together as possible. Or you might want to create a document, such as a contract, with extra space between the text lines so that you can write in your comments as you review it later.

WordPerfect provides many line spacing options, and you can change the line spacing in your document as often as you like. Follow these steps to change the line spacing in your document:

1. Move the cursor to the paragraph or position in the document where you want the change to take effect. If you want to change line spacing for the entire document, press Ctrl+Home to go to the top of the document. To change the line spacing for a block of text, select the text.

Line Space Changes in a Paragraph   No matter where you place the cursor in a paragraph, WordPerfect changes the line spacing from the beginning of that paragraph to the end of the document.

2. Open the Format menu and choose Line.

3. Select Spacing, and the Line Spacing dialog box appears, as shown in Figure 13.1.

Click these buttons to change line spacing.

FIGURE 13.1   The Line Spacing dialog box.

4. Type the new line spacing setting in the Spacing text box, or click the up or down arrow to increase or decrease the line spacing.

5. Click OK to enter the setting and return to the document screen. WordPerfect adjusts the line spacing accordingly.

TIP   **The Line Spacing Button**   To quickly change line spacing, place the cursor where you want the line spacing to be changed and click the Line Spacing button on the Power Bar and select the desired amount of spacing.

UNDERSTANDING JUSTIFICATION

Justification refers to how text is aligned on the page. As you type, WordPerfect justifies (aligns) the text against the left margin, leaving uneven lines at the right margin. You can change the alignment so that text is centered between the left and right margins, so that it lines up against the right margin (right-aligned), or that it lines up flush against both the left and right margins (fully justified). You can also use the Full and All justification options, which space the text evenly to produce even margins on both sides. (The difference between the two is that Full leaves the last line of a paragraph unjustified, while All justifies the last line.)

You can change the justification of text at any point in a document. Figure 13.2 shows paragraphs aligned using each of the available alignment options.

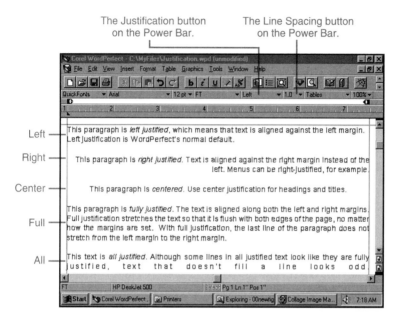

Figure 13.2   WordPerfect can justify text in several ways.

Changing Justification in a Document

If you want to change the justification for an existing section of text, select the text block (see Lesson 7 for help selecting text blocks) before you change the justification. If you change justification without first selecting a block of text, the new alignment remains in effect from the point where you changed it to the end of the document—or until WordPerfect finds another justification code in the document that tells it to change again.

These steps teach you how to change justification.

1. Position the cursor in the paragraph where you want to change the justification. If you want to change a block of text, select it now.

2. Open the Format menu and choose Justification. A submenu appears, listing the text alignment options.

3. Select the desired justification from the list, and Word-Perfect applies the new justification to your document.

 TIP **Power Justification** You can click the Justification button on the Power Bar and make a selection from that list to change the justification quickly.

In this lesson, you learned to set line spacing and change the justification of text. In the next lesson, you will learn how to view and change tab settings.

Setting Tabs

14

*In this lesson, you'll learn how to set
and clear tabs in WordPerfect.*

What Are Tabs?

Tabs are stop points that your cursor jumps to whenever you press
the Tab key. WordPerfect has preset tab stops every one-half inch.
You can use the tabs as they are, or you can change the settings.

Sometimes you may want to indent the first sentence in a paragraph. You may think that pressing the Spacebar several times to
move the text over is the same as pressing the Tab key once, but
there's a difference. Tabs move text an exact amount of space,
while spaces (created by pressing the Spacebar) move text an
amount that depends on the font and type of printer you have
selected. For example, if you are using proportionally spaced
fonts, such as Times New Roman (see Lesson 12), it is often im-
possible to line up a column of text or numbers by using the
Spacebar to move the cursor. Tabs enable you to move the cursor
to the same position for each line, which ensures that your tabbed
columns will be correctly aligned.

WordPerfect defines tabs in two ways:

- **Relative to the left margin** Relative tabs are set in
  relation to the left margin. If the left margin changes,
  WordPerfect adjusts the tabs to the new margin setting.
  For example, if you set a 2" relative tab with a 1" left margin, the actual position of the tab stop would be at 3".

- **Absolute to the left edge of the page** Absolute tabs
  are set in relation to the left edge of the physical page. For
  example, a 2" absolute tab setting would always remain 2"
  from the edge of the page regardless of the left margin.

The default tab setting is Relative, but you can set tabs either way.

VIEWING THE TAB STOP SETTINGS

Your current tab stops always appear on the Ruler Bar. If it is not already displayed, you can turn the Ruler Bar on by selecting View, Toolbars/Ruler and checking the Ruler Bar check box. WordPerfect displays tab stops in the form of triangles in the tabs area of the Ruler Bar (see Figure 14.1).

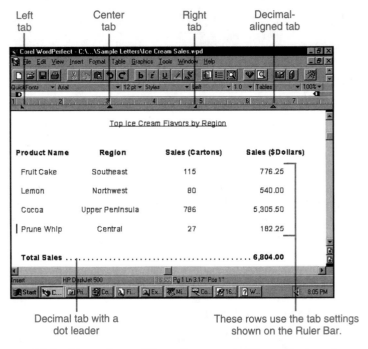

Figure 14.1 Text aligns differently around different types of tabs stops.

TYPES OF TAB STOPS

Which type of tab WordPerfect inserts when you press Tab depends on the current tab setting. You can choose from eight tab types: Left, Right, Center, and Decimal, each of which can also have a *leader*. The default tab setting is Left.

Leader A leader is a character used to fill spaces between items on a tabbed list. The most commonly used leaders are dots (periods) and hyphens.

Text aligns differently around each type of tab stop. Figure 14.1 shows how text aligns to different tab stop settings. The figure also shows the various symbols that are displayed on the Ruler Bar to represent the position and type of tab stops.

Left	The left edge of text aligns at the tab stop. (WordPerfect's default tab setting is left-aligned.)
Right	The right edge of text aligns at the tab stop.
Center	Text is centered around the tab stop.
Decimal-aligned	The decimal point (period) is aligned at the tab stop. When typing numbers, always set decimal-aligned tabs (called Deck tabs, for short). Your tabbed columns will align perfectly.

CLEARING TAB STOPS

It's best to work with only the tab settings you need. To clear a single tab stop, drag its Ruler Bar marker downward off the Ruler Bar.

If you prefer, you can clear all of the tab settings at one time, instead of dragging each one off the Ruler Bar. To do so, follow these steps:

1. Move the cursor to the beginning of the paragraph in the document where you want the tab stops to change.

2. Right-click the tabs area of the Ruler Bar to bring up the QuickMenu.

3. Select Clear All Tabs from the menu. WordPerfect immediately removes all tab stops.

Changing Tab Settings

When you change the tab settings, the new settings affect only the text from the point where you make the change. Therefore, it is extremely important to make sure that the cursor is positioned in the paragraph where you want the new settings to take effect.

To change tab settings, follow these steps:

1. Place the cursor in the paragraph where you want the new tab settings to take effect.

2. Place the mouse pointer in the tabs area of the Ruler Bar (see Figure 14.1) and right-click to access the QuickMenu.

3. Click Tab Set. The Tab Set dialog box appears, as shown in Figure 14.2.

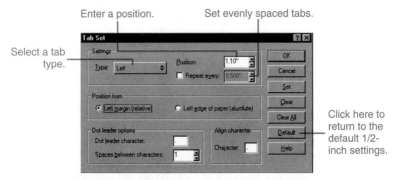

Figure 14.2 The Tab Set dialog box.

4. To delete a single tab setting, specify the setting in the Position text box and click Clear. To delete all existing tab settings, choose Clear all.

5. In the Position from area, choose whether you want to position the new tabs from the Left margin (relative) or from the Left edge of the paper (absolute).

6. Select a tab type from the Type drop-down list.

7. Specify a new tab setting in the Position text box and choose Set.

8. (Optional) If you have chosen a Leader tab, specify the character you want to use for the leader in the Dot leader character box.

9. When you finish setting tabs, click OK.

Whenever you create a new tab setting, WordPerfect inserts a tab icon into the left margin of your document (see Figure 14.3). To see the tab settings for the current paragraph, you can click that icon. A tab bar appears in your document so that you can see the tab settings and easily make changes to them by dragging the tab markers. As soon as you move the insertion point, the tab bar disappears.

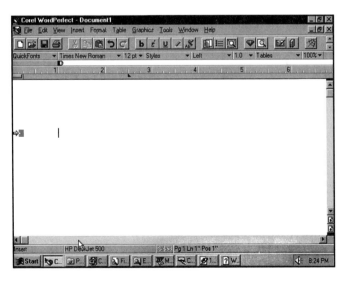

FIGURE 14.3 When you add a tab setting, WordPerfect displays a tab icon.

Put Down the Calculator   When you set tabs, you can type either decimals or fractions. For example, if you wanted to set a tab at 5 12/16", you could type the fraction, and WordPerfect would convert it to 5.75".

Setting Evenly Spaced Tabs

You can quickly set tab stops at regular intervals across the page by following these steps:

1. From the Tab Set dialog box (shown in Figure 14.2), click Clear All to clear all tabs.

2. Select a tab type from the Type drop-down list.

3. Enter the beginning tab setting in the Position text box, select Repeat every, and then specify the distance you want between tabs. (For example, you might want to repeat a tab every two inches.)

4. Click OK, and the Tab Set dialog box closes.

Changing the Tabs Back to Default Settings

Once you create new tab settings, you can easily return to the default settings of tabs at 1/2" intervals at a later position in your document. To return to default tab settings, follow these steps:

1. Position the cursor at the point where you want to change back to the default tab settings.

2. Right-click in the document window to access the QuickMenu.

3. Choose Default Tab Settings, and the document reverts back to default tab setting of left tabs at one-half-inch intervals.

SETTING TABS USING THE RULER BAR

Use the Ruler Bar to change tab settings if you want to change only a few tab settings in your document. (Of course, you have to make sure the Ruler Bar is displayed before you begin.) Change any tab setting from the Ruler Bar using one of these methods:

- To move an existing tab, click it and drag it to a new position. Release the mouse button, and WordPerfect realigns the text accordingly.

- To set a new tab, right-click the Ruler Bar in the position where you want the new tab. Then select the tab type from the QuickMenu that appears.

- To copy an existing tab, click it first and then press and hold down the Ctrl and Shift keys. WordPerfect displays a dotted vertical line to serve as a guide. Drag that guide to a new position, and then release the keys and the mouse button. WordPerfect places a copy of the original tab in the new location.

In this lesson, you learned about WordPerfect's tabs and how to set and clear them. In the next lesson, you will learn how to format paragraphs.

15

PARAGRAPH FORMATTING

In this lesson, you'll learn to format paragraphs with indents, QuickSpots, and QuickFormat.

WHAT IS A PARAGRAPH?

WordPerfect considers a paragraph to be amount of text that ends when you press Enter. A paragraph can be the title of a story, a report heading, or several sentences linked together to convey an idea or a thought. You can format each paragraph independently; almost like a mini-document within your document.

You can visually distinguish one paragraph from another in a number of ways.

- You can keep the entire paragraph flush with the left margin and simply press Enter twice at the end of the paragraph to leave a blank line between it and the next paragraph.

- You can press the Tab key before the first word of a paragraph to indent the first line to the first tab stop. Additional lines in the paragraph extend from the left margin to the right margin.

- You can *indent* an entire paragraph so that WordPerfect moves all of the lines of the paragraph to the first tab stop. To cancel or end the indented paragraph, you press Enter to begin another paragraph. The indent is canceled, and text you type in succeeding paragraphs appears at the left margin.

USING INDENTS

An *indent* is the space between the margin and the edge of a paragraph. WordPerfect provides four options for indenting paragraphs: left indent, double indent, hanging indent, and back tab (see Figure 15.1).

 Looks Are Deceiving! Don't try to create indents by using the Spacebar and the Enter key. Even though your paragraph may look okay on-screen, you won't be able to edit the paragraph later and keep the text lined up.

Left indent
Tabbed first line   Double indent

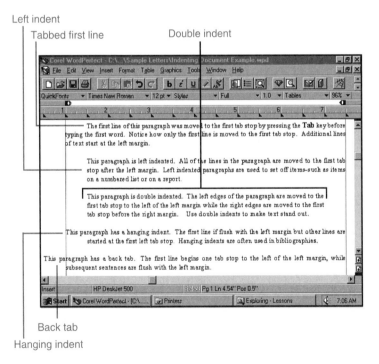

Back tab
Hanging indent

FIGURE 15.1 Types of indents.

To indent a paragraph or a block of selected paragraphs, follow these steps:

1. **Position the cursor in front of the first character of the paragraph you want to indent. If you want to indent a block of paragraphs instead, select them now.**

2. **Open the Format menu and choose Paragraph. A submenu appears.**

> **Quick Trick**   To create an indent using the QuickMenu, position the cursor at the first character of the paragraph you want to indent and right-click. Choose Indent to indent the paragraph.

3. **Select Indent, Double Indent, Hanging Indent, or Back Tab. WordPerfect indents the text accordingly.**

> **Indent from the Toolbar**   You can click the Indent button on the Toolbar to indent a paragraph one tab stop to the right. To make the button visible, drag the Toolbar into the document screen or display two rows of Toolbar buttons (as described in Lesson 2).

> **Back Tab**   You can use a back tab if you want to begin the first line of a paragraph one tab stop to the left of the left margin. To add a back tab, position the cursor in front of the first character of the paragraph where you want to insert a back tab and click the QuickSpot. (See the next section for more information about QuickSpots.) Choose Back Tab from the Indent drop-down list.

USING QUICKSPOTS

You've probably noticed the small gray square that appears in the left margin when the mouse pointer moves over a paragraph. WordPerfect calls these squares *QuickSpots*. QuickSpots provide quick access to frequently used paragraph options such as indent, justification, borders, fill, bullets, and font.

To use a QuickSpot, move the mouse pointer over the paragraph whose formatting you want to change and click the QuickSpot. WordPerfect selects the paragraph for you and opens the Paragraph dialog box, as shown in Figure 15.2. Click the drop-down arrow next to the desired paragraph feature to choose the appropriate formatting change. WordPerfect changes the paragraph format. When you finish making your changes, click the Close (X) button to close the dialog box.

FIGURE 15.2   Click a QuickSpot to open the Paragraph dialog box.

 Do It with Style!   WordPerfect comes with several paragraph styles, including several different Headings and bullets. Use the QuickSpot to add a style to your paragraph. Click Undo to reverse the style if it doesn't produce the effect you wanted.

USING QUICKFORMAT

QuickFormat offers an easy way to copy a paragraph style or font and attribute codes from one portion of your document to another. For example, you can add a Bullet Style to one paragraph and then quickly copy it to another paragraph. Or, you can change the font and attributes of one block of text and then copy the font and attributes to some other text.

Follow these steps to use QuickFormat:

1. Position the cursor anywhere in the paragraph that contains the formatting the style you want to copy. If you only want to copy the formatting from a specific portion of the paragraph, select that text only.

 2. Open the Format menu and choose QuickFormat, or click the QuickFormat button on the Toolbar. The QuickFormat dialog box appears, as shown in Figure 15.3.

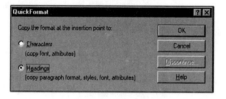

FIGURE 15.3   Use QuickFormat to copy formatting attributes.

3. Choose Characters to copy only the text formatting codes (such as bold or underline) and click OK. The mouse pointer changes to a paintbrush.

   or

   Choose Headings to copy the paragraph formatting (such as a style or a border and/or fill) in addition to text formatting codes. Then click OK. The mouse pointer changes to a paint roller.

4. Move the mouse pointer (now a paintbrush or paint roller) to the position where you want to copy the formatting or style.

5. If you chose Characters, drag the paintbrush across the text you want to change. As soon as you release the mouse button, the text is deselected and the new formatting takes effect. If you chose Headings, click anywhere in the paragraph where you want the new style to take effect.

6. (Optional) Repeat step 5 to copy the formatting or style to additional paragraphs.

7. When you're done copying the formatting or style, click the QuickFormat button on the Toolbar to turn off the feature. The mouse pointer returns to its normal shape.

In this lesson, you learned how to format paragraphs. In the next lesson, you'll learn how to set the paper size and margins.

SETTING THE PAGE SIZE AND MARGINS

In this lesson you'll learn how to set page sizes and margins for your document.

SELECTING THE PAGE SIZE

WordPerfect provides you with a standard 8 1/2-by-11-inch sheet of paper to print your document. You can fill as many of these sheets, or pages, as you'd like. If you want your document to print on another page size or type, such as custom stationery, you must select another *page definition*.

Page Definition   The page definition is a set of instructions about the page that WordPerfect sends to your printer. Along with the size and shape, definitions include information about the paper feed and source.

Although you can select many page sizes from the list, you can choose from only two types of page orientation: Portrait and Landscape. *Portrait* orientation prints text parallel to the short side of the page, which you might think of as a standard 8 1/2-by-11-inch sheet of paper. *Landscape* orientation prints text parallel to the long side of the page, which you might think of as an 11-by-8 1/2-inch sheet of paper.

Printer Dependent   Page definitions are entirely dependent on the printer you have selected. Because different printers support different options, some page sizes may not be available for your specific printer.

You can change the page size for the entire document or for selected pages. For example, if you were printing a four-page report on standard 8 1/2-by-11-inch paper, followed by a chart that fits on a 14-by-11-inch paper, you'd select a different page size and type for the chart.

Follow these steps to select a different page size:

1. Move the cursor to the page where you want to change the paper size. To change the paper size for all of the pages, press Ctrl+Home to move to the top of the document.

2. Open the Format menu and select Page. A submenu appears.

3. Select Page Size, and the Page Size dialog box appears, as shown in Figure 16.1.

Click to
open the
list and
select a
page size.

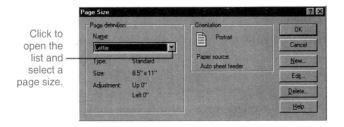

FIGURE 16.1   Select the correct page size from the Page Size dialog box.

4. Open the Name drop-down list and select the page size (such as Letter, Letter Landscape, Legal, or Legal Landscape, for example).

5. Click OK to return to the document screen.

TIP   **Changing Page Size from the Toolbar**   You can also click the Page Size button on the Toolbar to change the page size. To make the button visible, drag the Toolbar into the document window, or set WordPerfect to display two rows of Toolbar buttons. See Lesson 2 for details.

Default Settings If you want to print your document on a standard 8 1/2-by-11-inch page in portrait orientation, you do not have to select it. Because those are WordPerfect's default settings, they are already selected for you.

CREATING OR CHANGING A PAGE SIZE

You can create your own page definitions or edit existing ones. For example, you can create a page definition for printing on custom stationery. Follow these steps:

1. Open the Format menu and select Page. A submenu appears.

2. Select Page Size, and the Page Size dialog box appears.

3. To change an existing page size, select it from the Name drop-down list and click Edit. The Edit Page Size or the New Page Size dialog box appears (see Figure 16.2).

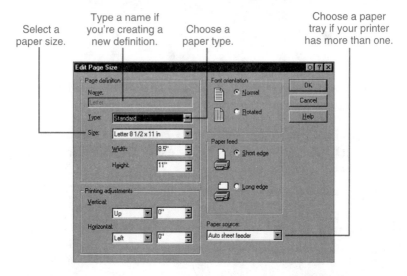

FIGURE 16.2   Change the page size with settings in the Edit Page Size dialog box.

4. Because not all page size options are supported by all printers, you may not be able to change some of the items in the dialog box. Follow any of these guidelines that apply to your printer.

- If you're setting up a new page size, you'll need to type a name in the Type text box.

- To indent the text on the page an additional amount from the margins, use the settings in the Printing adjustments area. For example, to lower the text an additional inch from the top of the page (to make room for preprinted letterhead, for example) set the Vertical (Down) adjustment to 1".

- Select Long edge in the Paper feed section if you want to feed the paper into the printer long-edge first.

5. Click OK to return to the Page Size dialog box.

6. The name of the page size you have edited or created appears in the Name box. Click OK to select the page size and return to your document.

SETTING PAGE MARGINS

Margins are the blank borders that extend from the top, bottom, left, and right edges of the page to the beginning of your text. WordPerfect's default margins are set at one inch. Therefore, the text you type appears one inch from the top, bottom, left, and right edges of each page.

You can change margins anywhere in your document. When you change the margins, the new settings affect all text from that point forward either to the end of the document or to the next code that changes the margins. You can change the left and right margins as many times as you want in your document. However, you can change the top and bottom margins only once on each page.

The following steps teach you how to change margins:

1. Use one of these methods to indicate the part of the document you want to change:

   - Move the cursor to the paragraph (for left and right margins) or to the page (top and bottom margins) where you want the change to begin.

   - If you want to change margins for the entire document, press Ctrl+Home to go to the top of the document.

   - To change the left or right margins for selected text only, select the text you want to change. (See Lesson 5 for help with selecting text.)

2. Open the Format menu and select Margins. The Margins dialog box shown in Figure 16.3 appears.

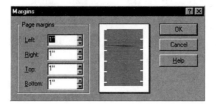

FIGURE 16.3 The Margins dialog box.

3. Click the up or down arrow next to the appropriate spin box to increase or decrease a margin setting, or type new settings (in inches) for the margins you want to change.

4. Click OK for the new settings to take effect.

Changing Margins from the Toolbar You can click the Page Margins button on the Toolbar to change the left, right, bottom, or top margins of a page. To make that button visible, drag the Toolbar into the document window, or set WordPerfect to display two rows of Toolbar buttons. See Lesson 2 for details.

Use the QuickMenu to Change Margins You can right-click in the left margin of the document and select Margins from the QuickMenu to open the Margins dialog box.

SETTING MARGINS USING THE RULER BAR

It's easy to change left and right margins in WordPerfect with the Ruler Bar. To display the Ruler Bar (if it's not already showing), open the View menu, select Toolbars/Ruler, and click the Ruler Bar check box to select it. Then follow these steps:

1. Move the cursor to the paragraph where you want the change to begin. Or, if you want to change margins for the entire document, press Ctrl+Home to go to the top of the document.

2. On the Ruler Bar, click the margin marker you want to change (see Figure 16.4).

Left margin marker   First line indent marker   Right margin marker

Left margin indent marker   Right margin indent marker

FIGURE 16.4 The Ruler Bar with indent and margin markers.

3. Hold the left mouse button down and drag to the desired location. When you release the mouse button, the margin changes.

In this lesson, you learned how to set the page size on which your document will print. You also learned how to change the left, right, top, and bottom margins for a document or a selected section. In the next lesson, you'll learn how to number your pages and add headers and footers.

17

WORKING WITH PAGE NUMBERS, HEADERS, AND FOOTERS

In this lesson, you'll learn how to add and remove page numbers, headers, and footers in your document. You'll also learn how to edit headers and footers.

ADDING PAGE NUMBERS

Although WordPerfect automatically keeps track of the increasing page count of your document, page numbers do not appear anywhere in the document unless you tell WordPerfect to show them. Follow these steps to display the page numbers:

1. Position the cursor on the first page where you want the page numbers to appear.

2. Open the Format menu and choose Page Numbering. A submenu appears.

3. Choose Select. The Select Page Numbering Format dialog box appears, as shown in Figure 17.1.

4. Open the Position drop-down list and select where you want the number to appear on each page.

5. Choose a page number format from the sample formats shown in the Page numbering format list box.

Select a position
for the page
number.

Choose a page
numbering format
from the samples.

Sample pages
show the result of
your selections.

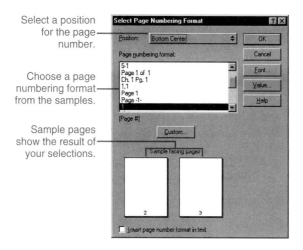

FIGURE 17.1   Choose how you want page numbers to look.

6. (Optional) Change the starting value of a page. (For example, if page 1 contains the cover page of a report and the text of the report actually begins on page 2, you might want WordPerfect to begin numbering on the second page of the document.) See the section below for more information.

7. Click OK to enter your settings and return to the document screen.

Count 'Em   Ever wonder how many total pages are in your document? Check the count at any time by choosing Format, Page Numbering, and Count Pages. A dialog box showing the current total page count appears. Click Close to return to the document screen.

Changing the Value of the Current Page Number

Someday you might need to begin page numbering other than on Page 1, or begin page numbering again at a new Page 1 later in your document. For example, you might want to number the first page of the main section of a report as "Page 1," even though it follows a table of contents and an introduction page. Perform these steps to change the value of the current page number and the rest of the pages to the end of the document:

1. Position the cursor on the first page where you want to change the value of the page number.

2. Open the Format menu and choose Page Numbering. A submenu appears.

3. Choose Value/Adjust. The Value/Adjust Number dialog box appears.

4. Click the Page tab, and then choose a Numbering Type such as 1,2,3 or A,B,C.

5. Type the starting page number value to appear on the current page (1, for example).

6. (Optional) Choose whether to always keep the page number the same or let the page number change as pages are added or deleted.

7. (Optional) Choose a Chapter, Volume, or Secondary page number by clicking the appropriate tab and entering the desired value.

8. Click Apply to add the page number values to your document and remain in the dialog box. Then click OK when you're ready to return to the document screen.

Controlling Page Breaks

As you type, WordPerfect determines where to *paginate* your document. When you add or delete text, WordPerfect automatically repaginates as necessary.

Paginate   To break the document into pages, based on the margins and other formatting options such as font size.

Sometimes you might want to change where WordPerfect starts a new page. For example, you might tell it to start a new page after a two-line title because even though the title page contains only a few lines of text, it needs to be on a separate page from the rest of the report.

To insert a page break, follow these steps:

1. Position the cursor at the location where you want to break the page.

2. Open the Insert menu and select Insert/Page Break, or press Ctrl+Enter. WordPerfect adds a page break and automatically repaginates the rest of the document.

TIP   **Page Break Codes**   When WordPerfect determines where to break the page, it places an [SPg] code in your document. The position of the [SPg] code can change as text is added or deleted. (To see the code, select View, Reveal Codes as covered in Lesson 11.) When you break a page yourself, WordPerfect places an [HPg] code in your document; this code remains constant even when text is added or deleted.

WHAT ARE HEADERS AND FOOTERS?

A *header* is text that appears at the top of a document page. A *footer* is text that appears at the bottom of a page. Headers and footers often contain such information as the page numbers, the chapter title, or the date.

You can set headers and footers to appear on every page or on odd or even pages, and you can suppress them on any page. (You might want to hide the header on the first page of a four-page memo, for example.) You can also create different headers and footers for the pages that will appear on the left and right sides of a bound document.

 Zero In   You use guidelines to control the exact placement of your header or footer. If guidelines are not already showing, turn them on by clicking View, Guidelines, checking the Header/Footer check box, and clicking OK. To turn guidelines off, repeat these steps.

CREATING HEADERS AND FOOTERS

Perform these steps to create either a header or footer:

1. Position the cursor on the first page where you want the header or footer to begin.

2. Open the Format menu and choose Header/Footer. The Headers/Footers dialog box appears, as shown in Figure 17.2.

FIGURE 17.2   The Headers/Footers dialog box.

3. Choose whether to create Header A, Header B, Footer A, or Footer B. (For now, choose the default Header A.)

TIP

A Quickie To access the Headers/Footers dialog box more quickly, right-click at the top of the page and choose Header/Footer from the resulting QuickMenu.

4. Click Create. The text on the page moves down to make room for the header. The title bar changes to show that you're editing a header, not the body of the document, and a Feature Bar appears (see Figure 17.3).

The title bar shows you're editing a header or footer.

Header/Footer Feature Bar

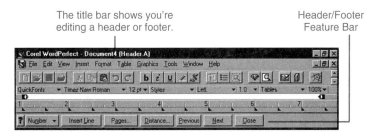

FIGURE 17.3 The Header/Footer Feature Bar gives you quick access to additional header and footer options.

 Feature Bar When you're working with features like headers and footers or tables and graphics, WordPerfect provides an extra row of buttons to help you with specific items for that feature.

5. Type the header or footer text. (It's best to limit your header to no more than three lines.)

6. (Optional) Add additional features, such as page numbers or graphic lines, using the Feature Bar. Table 17.1 describes each Feature Bar button.

7. When you finish typing your header or footer, click the Close button on the Feature Bar. You'll return to the document screen.

TABLE 17.1   BUTTONS ON THE HEADER/FOOTER FEATURE BAR

BUTTON	FUNCTION
Number	Inserts page numbers.
Insert Line	Inserts either horizontal or vertical lines to set off the text.
Pages	Specifies on which page (odd, even, or every page) the header or footer will appear.
Distance	Specifies the amount of space (in inches or percentages of inches) between the header and footer and the document text.
Previous	Jumps back to the previous header or footer in the document.
Next	Jumps ahead to the next header or footer in the document.
Close	Closes the Header/Footer Feature Bar and returns to the document screen.

 I Can't See It   If you're working in Draft mode, you won't be able to see page numbers, headers, or footers on your screen. To view them, open the View menu and choose Page or Two Page mode.

EDITING A HEADER OR FOOTER

Once you've created a header or footer, you can easily change it by following these steps:

1. Open the Format menu and choose Header/Footer. The Headers/Footers dialog box appears.

2. Select the header or footer you want to edit.

3. Click Edit. The Header or Footer you chose appears on-screen, along with the Header/Footer Feature Bar.

4. Make your changes.

5. When you finish editing your header or footer, click the Close button on the Feature Bar. You'll return to the document screen.

TURNING OFF HEADERS AND FOOTERS

You may want to discontinue the header or footer at some point in your document. For example, you may not want the header or footer to appear on the bibliography pages of a term paper. To turn off a header or footer, follow these steps:

1. Position the cursor in the page where you want to turn off the header or footer.

2. Open the Format menu and select Header/Footer.

3. Click Discontinue. The header or footer is discontinued from this page forward.

To suppress page numbers and/or headers or footers for a single page (such as a cover page), follow these steps:

1. Place your cursor on the page where you want to suppress the feature.

2. Open the Format menu, choose Page, and choose Suppress. The Suppress dialog box appears.

3. Select the items you want to suppress and click OK.

In this lesson, you learned how to add and remove page numbers and headers and footers. In the next lesson, you'll learn how to create a bulleted or numbered list.

18 LESSON

CREATING NUMBERED AND BULLETED LISTS

In this lesson, you'll learn how to create different types of lists.

CREATING A BULLETED OR NUMBERED LIST

A list organizes information for a reader. WordPerfect enables you to create three types of lists:

- A collection of points in no particular order
- A collection of points preceded by a bullet character
- A collection of numbered points (which must be in a specific order)

The first type of list is a generic list of items, each of which appears on its own line. To create such a list, you simply type each item and press Enter to go to the next line.

A bulleted list is an effective tool for emphasizing points that do not have a specific order. WordPerfect provides you with many bullet styles to choose from. Numbered lists are effective for listing points in order of importance and for creating a series of numbered steps.

Follow these steps to create a bulleted or numbered list:

1. Position the cursor in the place where you want to begin the list.

2. Open the Insert menu and choose Bullets and Numbers. The Bullets & Numbers dialog box appears, as shown in Figure 18.1.

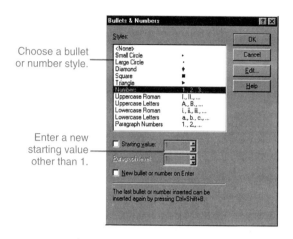

Choose a bullet
or number style.

Enter a new
starting value
other than 1.

FIGURE 18.1   The Bullets & Numbers dialog box.

3. Select a bullet or number style from the Styles list.

4. (Optional) To change the starting number in a numbered
list, check the Starting value check box and enter a number.

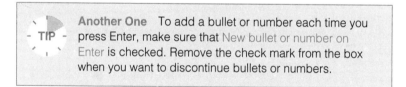

Another One   To add a bullet or number each time you
press Enter, make sure that New bullet or number on
Enter is checked. Remove the check mark from the box
when you want to discontinue bullets or numbers.

5. Click OK. The dialog box closes, and a bullet or number
appears on the document screen.

6. Type the text for the first item and press Enter.

7. To add additional bulleted or numbered items, press
Ctrl+Shift+B or click the Insert Bullet button on the
WordPerfect 7 Toolbar.

> **TIP** **QuickMenu Bullets and Numbers** To quickly add a bullet or number, position the mouse pointer in the document and right-click to access the QuickMenu. Choose Bullets to open the Bullets & Numbers dialog box.

ADDING ITEMS TO AND REMOVING ITEMS FROM A NUMBERED LIST

It's easy to add items to a numbered list. If you insert an item between numbered items, WordPerfect correctly numbers the new item and then renumbers the entire list from the new item to the end of the list.

Follow these steps to add a numbered item to an existing list:

1. Position the cursor at the end of the line *directly before* the place you want to insert a new item.

2. Press Enter to insert a new line. WordPerfect automatically inserts the new list number and renumbers the rest of the list.

Follow these steps to remove a numbered item from an existing list:

1. Select the numbered item you want to delete (as described in Lesson 6).

2. Press Delete to delete the highlighted item. WordPerfect automatically renumbers the remaining items on the list.

By default, whenever you type a number, letter, or character followed by an indent, a tab, or a space at the beginning of a line, WordPerfect automatically sets up a numbered list for you using a QuickCorrect option called Format-As-You-Go. (See Lesson 5 for more information on QuickCorrect.) If you'd rather create a bulleted list, or if you don't want to create a list at all, you can turn off Format-As-You-Go options at any time.

To turn off the Format-As-You-Go option that automatically adds bullets (or any other Format-As-You-Go option), follow these steps:

1. Open the Tools menu and choose QuickCorrect. WordPerfect displays the QuickCorrect dialog box.

2. In the QuickCorrect dialog box, choose Options. The QuickCorrect options shown in Figure 18.2 appear.

3. At the bottom of the dialog box is a section entitled QuickCorrect Format-As-You-Go options. In the Item list, deselect QuickBullets.

Deselect any Format-As-You-Go option.

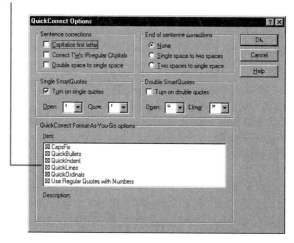

FIGURE 18.2   Use these options to control the Format-As-You-Go feature.

In this lesson, you learned how to create both bulleted and numbered lists and how to add and delete list items. In the next lesson, you'll learn how to create columns.

19 CREATING COLUMNS

In this lesson, you'll learn how to create columns for use in newsletters, charts, and reports.

UNDERSTANDING WORDPERFECT COLUMNS

As you type, the text in a normal document appears in one column that extends from the left margin to the right margin. If you prefer, you can break the text into smaller columns. Multiple columns are often used in newsletters, reports, and charts because they present text in an easy-to-read format.

You can create columns anywhere in your WordPerfect document and still revert back to normal one-column text wherever it's more appropriate. By default, WordPerfect leaves 1/2 inch of white space (called a *gutter*) between columns, and the columns all have the same width.

There are two main types of columns: *newspaper* and *parallel*, both of which are shown in Figure 19.1.

- Newspaper columns contain text that flows down the length of one column on a page and then wraps to the top of the next column on the same page just like your daily newspaper.

  Balanced Newspaper columns are similar to newspaper columns, but if the two columns of text do not fill a page, the amount of text in each column is adjusted to make them as close to the same length as possible.

- Parallel columns contain short blocks of text placed side by side in rows (like in a table). Parallel columns are used in itineraries, for example. They can be set up as regular or *block protected.*

Parallel Columns with Block Protect are parallel columns to which block protection is applied. When you use these columns, the entire column is bumped to the next page if all of its lines won't fit on the same page.

Block Protect A feature that keeps specified text blocks on the same page.

Parallel columns | Newspaper columns

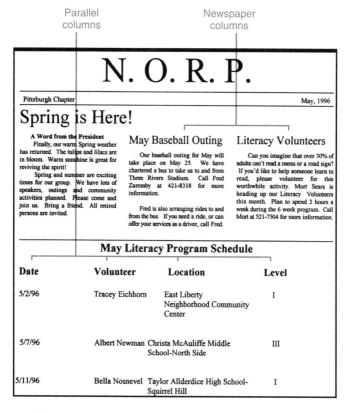

N. O. R. P.

Pittsburgh Chapter | May, 1996

Spring is Here!

A Word from the President

Finally, our warm Spring weather has returned. The tulips and lilacs are in bloom. Warm sunshine is great for reviving the spirit!

Spring and summer are exciting times for our group. We have lots of speakers, outings and community activities planned. Please come and join us. Bring a friend. All retired persons are invited.

May Baseball Outing

Our baseball outing for May will take place on May 25. We have chartered a bus to take us to and from Three Rivers Stadium. Call Fred Zaremby at 421-8318 for more information.

Fred is also arranging rides to and from the bus. If you need a ride, or can offer your services as a driver, call Fred.

Literacy Volunteers

Can you imagine that over 30% of adults can't read a menu or a road sign? If you'd like to help someone learn to read, please volunteer for this worthwhile activity. Mort Sears is heading up our Literacy Volunteers this month. Plan to spend 2 hours a week during the 6 week program. Call Mort at 521-7504 for more information.

May Literacy Program Schedule

Date	Volunteer	Location	Level
5/2/96	Tracey Eichhorn	East Liberty Neighborhood Community Center	I
5/7/96	Albert Newman	Christa McAuliffe Middle School-North Side	III
5/11/96	Bella Nosnevel	Taylor Allderdice High School-Squirrel Hill	I

FIGURE 19.1 A newsletter and accompanying schedule using newspaper and parallel columns.

Defining Columns in Your Document

WordPerfect enables you to define columns in two ways: you can select existing text and define columns for that text only, or you can define the columns and then add text to them. With the latter method, once you've defined the columns, all text you type takes the column format from that point forward until you either change the column layout or turn off the column feature.

When working with columns, you'll probably want to display the Ruler Bar because it shows column markers (see Figure 19.2). To turn on the Ruler Bar display, open the View menu, select Toolbars/Ruler, and click Ruler Bar.

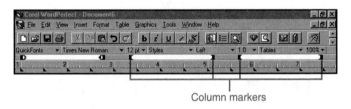

Column markers

Figure 19.2   The Ruler Bar shows where your columns are set.

Perform these steps to define columns:

1. Position the cursor at the point in your document where you want the columns to begin. (If you want to format a block of existing text as columns, select the text first and then follow steps 2–7.)

2. Open the Format menu and choose Columns. A submenu appears.

3. Select Define. The Columns dialog box appears, as shown in Figure 19.3.

4. Type the number of columns you want in the Number of columns spin box, or click the up or down arrow to increase or decrease the number shown.

5. Select a column type.

6. (Optional) Adjust the values in the Spacing between columns and Column width spin boxes, if necessary.

7. Click OK, and WordPerfect displays all text from that point forward in columns.

Select the number of columns you want.

Select a column type.

Column width is set automatically.

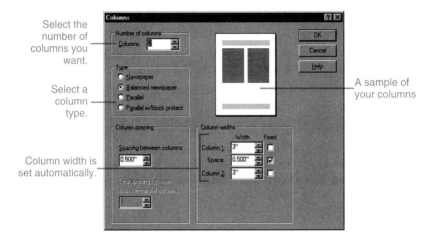

A sample of your columns

FIGURE 19.3 The Columns dialog box.

TIP   Fixed Width   WordPerfect adjusts all column widths to make sure they fit across a page. Click the Fixed check box for any particular column for which you want to ensure that the width won't be changed if you adjust other columns.

ENTERING TEXT INTO COLUMNS

After you have defined your columns, you simply type text as usual. When the text in a newspaper style column reaches the bottom of a page, it flows to the top of the next column. To type text into another column, insert a column break by pressing

Ctrl+Enter. Once you have entered text into columns, you move around by clicking in the column you want to move to.

 TIP **Column Widths** To quickly modify any column width, drag the column margin marker on the Ruler Bar.

TURNING OFF COLUMNS

It's easy to turn the column feature off at any point in your document. These steps show you how.

1. Open the Format menu and choose Columns.

2. From the submenu, select Off. WordPerfect inserts into your document a hidden code that turns the columns off. (To learn more about WordPerfect's hidden codes, see Lesson 11.) Text that follows the ending code flows normally from the left margin to the right.

 TIP **Adding Borders,Lines, and Fills** To make a column stand out, you can add a border, line, or fill. To do so, click inside the desired column and then choose Format, Border/Fill, and Columns. Select a border and fill style and click OK. For more help with borders, see Lesson 21.

In this lesson, you learned how to create and modify columns. In the next lesson, you will learn how to work with tables.

WORKING WITH TABLES

20

In this lesson, you will learn how to create and format tables. You'll also learn how to sum a table column.

WHAT IS A TABLE?

You can use tables in place of tabbed columns when the columns vary in length. Tables work much like spreadsheets, providing an easy way to create financial reports or invoices like the one shown in Figure 20.1. Tables are one of WordPerfect's most versatile features. Once you learn how to work with the Table feature, you'll come up with many of your own uses for a table!

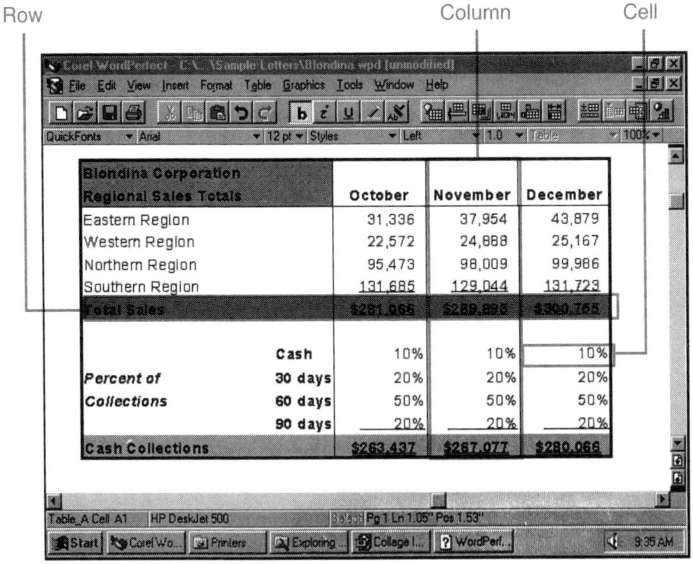

Row   Column   Cell

FIGURE 20.1 A WordPerfect table.

A table consists of horizontal *rows* and vertical *columns*. The inter-section of a row and a column forms a rectangular box called a *cell*. Each cell can contain text, numbers, or a combination of text and numbers.

CREATING A TABLE

Creating a table is a snap. Follow these steps:

1. Position your cursor at the place you want to create the table.

> **Drag Magic**   Create a table quickly by clicking the Tables button on the Power Bar. Drag the mouse over the table grid to fill in the desired number of rows and columns. When you've selected the number of rows and columns you want, release the mouse button to insert the table into your document.

2. Open the Table menu and choose Create. The Create Table dialog box appears, as shown in Figure 20.2.

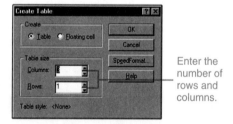

Enter the number of rows and columns.

FIGURE 20.2   The Create Table dialog box.

3. Enter the number of rows and columns you want in the Rows and Columns spin boxes.

4. Click OK to close the dialog box and return to the document screen. The table appears on-screen according to your specifications, with your cursor in the top left cell (cell A1).

When you create a table, WordPerfect automatically replaces the WordPerfect 7 Toolbar (displayed by default) with the Tables Toolbar. As soon as you're done with the table, the WordPerfect 7 Toolbar reappears.

TIP **Table QuickMenu** The Table QuickMenu contains most of the commands available on the Table menu. To access the Table QuickMenu, right-click inside the table.

MOVING AROUND AND TYPING TEXT IN A TABLE

To enter information into a cell, you click in the cell and begin typing. You can type, edit, and format your text as you would text in any regular paragraph. If your text is too long to fit in the width of the cell, WordPerfect wraps the text to the next line and enlarges the height of the cell accordingly.

The easiest way to move around in a table is to click in the cell you want to move to. However, as you begin typing information into the table's cells, you may find that using the keyboard to move from cell to cell is easier and faster. Table 20.1 provides the most common shortcut keys you can use to move around in your table.

TIP **Extra Help** Click the Row/Column indicators button on the Tables Toolbar to display the row numbers and column letters. Seeing the indicators on-screen helps you keep track of your location!

TABLE 20.1   TABLE MOVEMENT KEYS

TO MOVE...	PRESS...
To the next cell	Tab
To the previous cell	Shift+Tab
One cell down	Alt+↓
One cell up	Alt+↑

As you move around in the table, notice that WordPerfect keeps track of your location and displays the current cell name on the first button on the Status Bar.

TIP   **Enter Not**   Unless you want to create a new line in a cell, be careful not to press Enter as you are typing text in the table.

CHANGING THE TABLE'S SIZE AND APPEARANCE

Once you've created your table, you can make many changes to the way the table looks. In addition to adding regular text formatting, you can adjust column widths or row heights, remove the table's separator lines, and add shading to selected cells or the entire table.

USING SPEEDFORMAT

You can let WordPerfect automatically format the table with the SpeedFormat feature. Click the SpeedFormat button on the Tables Toolbar, or open the Table menu and choose the SpeedFormat command. From the list of styles that appears, select a style. The sample table changes to match your selection. When you find a style you like, click Apply to apply it to your table.

ADDING OR DELETING ROWS AND COLUMNS

If your cursor is in the last cell of the table, you can press Tab to insert a new row. In all other cases, follow these steps to add rows and/or columns to your table.

1. Position the cursor where you want to add a row or column.

2. Open the Table menu, choose Insert, and select Row or Column from the submenu. The Insert Columns/Rows dialog box appears (see Figure 20.3).

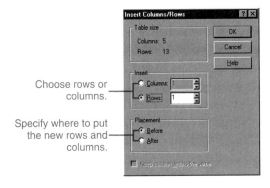

Choose rows or columns.

Specify where to put the new rows and columns.

FIGURE 20.3 The Insert Columns/Rows dialog box.

3. Select Rows or Columns, and then enter the number of rows or columns you want to insert.

4. Select Before or After to indicate where you want to insert the rows or columns in relation to the current row or column.

5. Click OK. The dialog box closes, and WordPerfect adds the rows or columns to your table.

Row Shortcut Press Alt+Insert to insert a row before the cursor. Press Alt+Shift+Insert to insert a row after the cursor. Press Alt+Delete to delete the current row.

To delete rows or columns, first select the rows or columns you want to delete. Then open the Table menu and choose Delete. In the Delete dialog box, select the rows or columns you want to delete (or choose Cell contents or Formulas only) and click OK. You're returned to the table, and the rows or columns are gone.

ADJUSTING THE WIDTH OF COLUMNS

When you create a table, WordPerfect makes the table as wide as the page width and sets the columns to equal widths. You can adjust a column's width by following these steps:

1. If the Ruler Bar is not already showing, select View, Toolbars/Ruler, and click Ruler Bar.

2. The inverted triangles on the Ruler Bar (see Figure 20.4) represent the table's column separators. Drag the triangle of the column you want to adjust. (Notice that a dotted guide helps you position the column separator.)

Drag an inverted triangle
marker to adjust the
column's width.

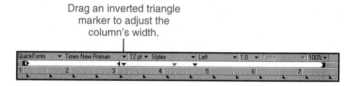

FIGURE 20.4 You can change the width of any column.

3. When the dotted line shows the desired width, release the mouse button. WordPerfect adjusts the column width accordingly.

TIP **Size to Fit** To adjust a column width to accommodate the widest entry in the column, position the cursor anywhere in the column and click the Size Column to Fit button on the Tables Toolbar.

CHANGING LINES OR FILLS

Normally, each cell in a table is bordered all four sides by a single line. However, you can change the line to another style, or you can turn the lines off completely.

Figure 20.1 shows examples of some of the shading and line styles you can use in your tables. To change the line style or shading of cells, follow these steps:

1. Select the cells whose lines you want to change.

 2. Click the Lines/Fill button on the Tables Toolbar. (You can also choose this command from the Table menu.) The Properties for Table Lines/Fill dialog box appears.

3. In the Properties for Table Lines/Fill dialog box, select cell line styles, cell line colors, and fill options for the selected cells or the entire table.

4. When you finish changing the options, click OK. You are returned to the document, where you'll see that your changes are now in effect.

 Change the Table   To change the line style or shading for the entire table, position your cursor in any cell of the table and click the Lines/Fill button on the Tables Toolbar. Click the Table tab in the resulting dialog box and choose a table border, default cell lines, and fill options. Click OK to return to the document and see the changes.

JOINING AND SPLITTING CELLS

You can join (combine) multiple adjacent cells or split a large cell into smaller cells. For example, you might want to combine all of the cells in the first table row to make them into one cell in which you can type the heading for the table.

Select the cells you want to join, open the Table menu, select Join, and click Cell. To split a cell into smaller cells, select the cell to split, open the Table menu, select Split, and select Cell. Enter the number of rows or column you want to split the cell into and click OK.

Numbers Options

Because WordPerfect tables are similar to spreadsheet programs in many ways, WordPerfect enables you to type numbers and enter formulas in your table. Tables offer the capability of adding mathematical functions and formulas to your document.

To format numbers in your tables, select the cells you want to format and then click the Numeric Format button on the Tables Toolbar. Choose a number type (such as currency or commas) from the dialog box that appears, and click OK.

Summing a Table Column

One of the most exciting things about working with a WordPerfect table is that you can quickly sum a column of numbers. The easiest way to do this is to total a vertical column using two simple steps:

1. Position the cursor in the cell where you want the sum to appear.

2. Open the Table menu and choose QuickSum or press Ctrl+=. WordPerfect inserts a formula in the cell, and the total of all the preceding numbers in the column appears.

 Calculate If you change one of the numbers in the column, the total for that column will not automatically reflect the change. To update a formula's result, click the Calculate button, and then click the Calc Table button in the Calculate dialog box.

In this lesson, you learned to use WordPerfect's Table feature. In the next lesson, you'll learn how to dress up your document.

DRESSING UP YOUR DOCUMENT

In this lesson, you'll learn various ways to dress up your document.

ADDING A DROP CAP

A *drop cap* is a large first letter of a paragraph that is sometimes used to begin a chapter or first page. Drop caps decorate a page and catch your eye. Perform these steps to add a drop cap with WordPerfect:

1. Place the cursor anywhere in the paragraph in which you want to add a drop cap.

2. Open the Format menu and choose Drop Cap. The Drop Cap Feature Bar appears, as shown in Figure 21.1.

3. (Optional) Use the Feature Bar buttons to customize the drop cap. Table 21.1 describes each Feature Bar button.

TIP

No Need to Select You don't have to select the first letter of a paragraph when adding a drop cap to text you've already typed. WordPerfect automatically selects the first letter of the paragraph, increases its size, and wraps the other text around it.

TABLE 21.1   **DROP CAP FEATURE BAR BUTTONS**

BUTTON	USE IT TO...
Type	Choose a predefined drop cap style
Size	Change the drop cap's size
Position	Adjust the exact placement of the drop cap
Font	Change the drop cap's font
Border/Fill	Add a border and/or fill to the drop cap
Options	Choose how many characters (or even the whole first word) to include in the drop cap
Close	Close the Drop Cap Feature Bar

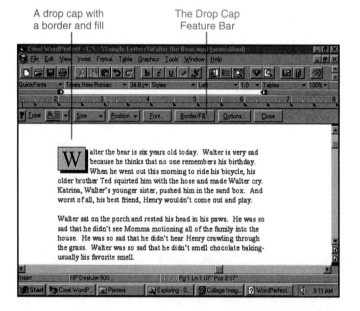

FIGURE 21.1   Adding a drop cap adds excitement to the page.

USING WORDPERFECT CHARACTERS

WordPerfect allows you to add more than 2,500 special characters to your document. WordPerfect's characters are organized in character sets and include symbols that range from smiley faces to Cyrillic alphabet letters. These characters are just like any normal text characters; you can insert them anywhere in your document. Figure 21.2 shows some of the special characters you can use.

☞ **If you check the Area Code first, you can ✄ the ☺ it takes to ☎ home!**

☺☺☺☺

FIGURE 21.2   You can insert special characters anywhere in your document.

Follow these steps to add WordPerfect characters to your document:

1. Position the cursor where you want to insert the character.

2. Open the Insert menu and choose Character. The WordPerfect Characters dialog box appears, as shown in Figure 21.3.

Choose a
character set.

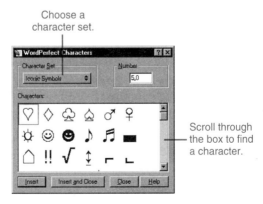

Scroll through
the box to find
a character.

FIGURE 21.3   The WordPerfect Characters dialog box.

3. Choose a character set from the Character Set list.

4. Click any character to select it.

5. To insert the character into your document and keep the WordPerfect Characters dialog box open, click Insert.

or

To insert the character into your document and close the dialog box, click Insert and Close.

I Changed My Mind   You can click Close at any time to close the WordPerfect Characters dialog box and return to the document screen.

Quick Characters   When the cursor's positioned in the location where you want to insert a character, you can right-click and choose Character from the QuickMenu.

CENTERING TEXT ON A PAGE

Centering text between the top and bottom margins is an effective visual aid when you have only a small amount of text on a page. Text can be centered for the current page or for the current page and following pages. Vertically centered text is useful when you are creating the title page of a report or an invitation, for example.

Follow these steps to center text between the top and bottom margins of a page:

1. Position the cursor on the page where you want to center the text.

2. Open the Format menu and choose Page. The Center Page(s) dialog box appears, as shown in Figure 21.4.

FIGURE 21.4 The Center Page(s) dialog box.

3. Choose one of the following options:

Current page centers only the current page.

Current and subsequent pages centers all pages beginning at the cursor position.

No centering tells WordPerfect to stop centering pages as a result of the Current and subsequent pages option.

4. Click OK to return to the document screen.

ADDING A BORDER

You can use a page border to add excitement to any document. Borders and *fills* set off title pages, charts, and flyers. You can add borders to full pages or selected paragraphs.

A page border runs from the top margin to the bottom margin and from the left margin to the right margin. When you use a page border, WordPerfect automatically inserts space between the text margins and the border so that the text is not too crowded.

 Fill Shading that is placed behind text, usually to add emphasis. For example, this box contains a fill.

Follow these steps to add a page border:

1. Place the cursor anywhere in the page to which you want to add a border.

2. Open the Format menu and choose Border/Fill.

3. Select Page from the submenu that appears. The Page
Border/Fill dialog box appears, as shown in Figure 21.5.

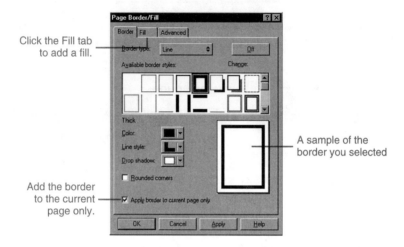

Click the Fill tab to add a fill.

A sample of the border you selected

Add the border to the current page only.

FIGURE 21.5   Make a page exciting by adding a border.

4. From the Border type list, select Line or Fancy.

5. If you choose Line, select the type of border you want
from the Available border styles area.

6. (Optional) Use the Color, Line style, and Drop shadow list
boxes and the Rounded corners check box to further enhance your border. A sample of the selected line style
appears in the sample box (see Figure 21.5).

TIP   **Fancy Fun**   To add extra oomph to a document, select
Fancy as the border type and experiment with some of
the many available choices. If your printer supports color
printing, the colored borders will print in color.

7. Click the Apply border to current page only check box to
add the border to this page only.

8. (Optional) To change foreground or background colors or to adjust the fill pattern, click the Fill tab and choose from the available fill styles.

9. Click Apply to add the border. Then click OK to return to the document screen.

ADDING A BORDER TO A PARAGRAPH

If you want, you can add a border to selected paragraphs instead of to a whole page. To place a border around a paragraph, follow these steps:

1. Position the cursor within the paragraph to which you want to add a border. (See Lesson 6 for details on selecting text.)

2. Open the Format menu and choose Border/Fill.

3. Select Paragraph from the submenu that appears. The Paragraph Border/Fill dialog box appears.

4. Follow steps 4–9 in the previous section to add the paragraph border.

 Not So Fancy   You can add only line borders to a selected paragraph. WordPerfect does not make Fancy borders available for paragraphs.

 Just a Tad   You can select any paragraph on the page(s) and add a border around it. To do so, select the text, open the Format menu, and select Border/Fill.

USING HIGHLIGHT

Highlight places a colored bar over selected text. Highlights are often used to draw attention to important parts of a document, such as a chapter title or heading. You can use several highlight colors in the same document.

Follow these steps to add a highlight:

1. Select the text you want to highlight.

2. Click the Highlight Toolbar button, and the highlight appears across the selected text.

Highlight Colors To change the color of the highlight, **TIP** open the Tools menu, select Highlight, and select Change Color. Choose a new color from the drop-down list and click OK.

In this lesson, you learned how to dress up your document by adding drop caps, WordPerfect characters, and page and paragraph borders. You also learned how to center text on a page and highlight text. In the next lesson, you'll learn how to find and replace text.

FINDING AND REPLACING TEXT

*In this lesson, you'll learn how to find text or codes
in your document and how to replace them, if desired, with other
text or codes.*

FINDING A TEXT STRING

WordPerfect can search through your entire document or any
selected portion of the document to locate any text. You can
search for a single character, a word, or a phrase, and you can
search from top to bottom or bottom to top. (If you want to replace the word or phrase with something else, refer to the section
"Replacing Text or Codes" later in this lesson.) To find text,
follow these steps:

1. Position the cursor where you want the search to begin.
   (Press Ctrl+Home to start from the beginning of the document.)

2. Open the Edit menu and choose Find and Replace. The
   Find and Replace Text dialog box appears, as shown in
   Figure 22.1.

3. In the Find text box, type the search string, which can be
   up to 80 characters long.

Search String   The character, word, or text phrase you
want WordPerfect to look for.

Pull-down menus help you conduct your search.

Type the text you're looking for here.

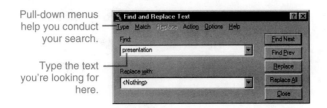

Figure 22.1   The Find and Replace Text dialog box.

4. (Optional) For a more detailed search, select one of the following options from the pull-down menus in the Find and Replace Text dialog box:

- Open the Type menu and select Word Forms to tell WordPerfect to find any form of the word you're looking for. For example, if you type "jump," WordPerfect finds "jumped," "jumping," and "jumps."

- Open the Match menu and choose specific criteria that you want to match, such as the same text case (lower- or uppercase), a whole word, or a specific font.

- Open the Action menu and choose where you want WordPerfect to place the cursor in relation to the text string it finds. The default is to have Word-Perfect select (highlight) the found text; but you can change it to have the program place the cursor be-fore or after the string, or extend the selection to include words next to the string.

- Open the Options menu and choose where in the document to search (such as from the top of the document downward and/or in headers and footers).

5. Click Find Next to begin the search. WordPerfect moves to the first occurrence of the word or phrase. (The Find and Replace Text dialog box remains on the screen.)

6. Repeat step 5 if necessary to move to the next occurrence of the word or phrase.

7. (Optional) Click Find Prev to move to the previous occurrence of the word or phrase.

8. Click Close to close the dialog box and return to the document.

SEARCHING FOR HIDDEN CODES

In Lesson 11, you learned that WordPerfect inserts hidden codes into your document to record formatting changes. In addition to searching for text, you can find these hidden codes. For example, if you want to see each tab setting you've added, you can search for the tab set code.

To search for a code, follow these steps:

1. Position the cursor where you want the search to begin.

2. Open the Reveal Codes window by right-clicking in the document window and choosing Reveal Codes from the QuickMenu.

3. Open the Edit menu and choose Find and Replace. The Find and Replace Text dialog box appears.

4. Open the Match menu in the dialog box and choose Codes. The Codes dialog box appears (see Figure 22.2).

5. Scroll through the list, select the code you want to find in the document, and click Insert. (If this is the only code you'll be searching for, click Insert and Close.)

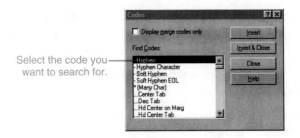

Select the code you want to search for.

FIGURE 22.2 The Codes dialog box.

6. (Optional) If you want to search for side-by-side codes (such as [Bold][Und]), repeat step 4 to add other codes to the Find text box.

7. When you finish adding codes, click Close to close the Codes dialog box and return to the Find and Replace Text dialog box. Click Find Next to start the search.

8. (Optional) Click Find Next again to continue searching for other occurrences of the code.

9. When you finish searching, click Close.

 Don't Type It! Even though it looks like you could type the code in the Find and Replace Text dialog box, WordPerfect will treat a typed code like text. You must select codes from the Match menu to find them in your document.

REPLACING TEXT OR CODES

Find and Replace allows you to replace a word, phrase, or hidden code with another word, phrase, or code, or to completely remove the item it finds. For example, you could replace the word "traveling" with the word "flying," or you could replace a [Bold] code with <Nothing> to remove the bold attribute.

Follow these steps to replace text and/or codes:

1. Position the cursor where you want the find and replace procedure to begin. You can search from top to bottom or bottom to top. (Press Ctrl+Home to start from the beginning of the document.)

2. Open the Edit menu and choose Find and Replace. The Find and Replace Text dialog box appears, as shown in Figure 22.3.

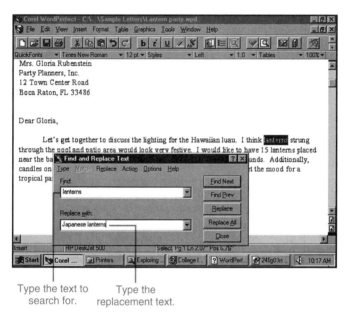

Type the text to search for.   Type the replacement text.

FIGURE 22.3   Find text and replace it with other text.

3. In the Find text box, type the text you want to replace. If you want to replace a code, open the Match menu, choose Codes, and select a code as described in the previous section.

4. In the Replace with text box, type the replacement text. To select a replacement code, select Match, Codes and select a code according to the earlier instructions.

TIP

Do Nothing If you want to replace text or codes with nothing (essentially deleting them), do not enter anything in the Replace with text box. WordPerfect inserts **<Nothing>** in the Replace with text box by default.

5. (Optional) For a more detailed search and replace operation, select one of the following options from the pull-down menus in the Find and Replace dialog box:

- Open the Type menu and select Word Forms to tell WordPerfect to find any form of the word you're looking for. For example, if you type "jump," WordPerfect finds "jumped," "jumping," and "jumps."

- Open the Replace menu and choose specific details that you want to match, such as the same text case (lower- or uppercase), a whole word, or a specific font.

Why Can't I Select Replace? Your cursor must be in the Replace with text box for the Replace menu to be active.

- Open the Action menu and choose where you want WordPerfect to place the cursor in relation to the text string it finds. The default is to have Word-Perfect select (highlight) the found text; but you can change it to have the program place the cursor before or after the string, or extend the selection to include words next to the string.

- Open the Options menu and choose where in the document to search (such as from the top of the document downward and/or in headers and footers).

6. Click Replace to replace the first occurrence of the found word or code and advance to the next one, or click Replace All to replace all occurrences throughout the document. If WordPerfect does not find any occurrence of the word or code, it notifies you accordingly.

7. Click Close when the Find and Replace operation is complete to close the dialog box and return to the document.

In this lesson, you learned how to find specific text or hidden codes in your document and how to replace them with other text or codes or to remove them entirely. In the next lesson, you'll learn how to use WordPerfect's writing tools.

LESSON 23

USING WORDPERFECT'S WRITING TOOLS

In this lesson, you will learn how to use WordPerfect's spelling, grammar, and thesaurus tools.

CHECKING YOUR SPELLING

WordPerfect has two spelling features: Spell-As-You-Go and Spell Checker. Spell-As-You-Go functions as a proofreader that watches for errors as you type your document. The Spell Checker program hunts for spelling errors and provides possible corrections. Spell Checker checks your words against its main dictionary. You can add any word to the dictionary so that WordPerfect won't stop on it again.

USING SPELL-AS-YOU-GO

Spell-As-You-Go checks your spelling as you type. WordPerfect automatically turns on Spell-As-You-Go when you enter the program, but you can turn it off any time. Spell-As-You-Go marks words that might be misspelled with a red squiggly underline. To correct a misspelled word, follow these steps:

1. Right-click in the misspelled word, and a list of possible replacement words appears.

2. Select the correct spelling from the list. WordPerfect replaces the misspelled word with the correct word you selected.

Add Words If you frequently use a word such as a
name or a foreign word that WordPerfect marks as misspelled, click Add to add it to the WordPerfect dictionary.

It Thinks Everything Is an Error! If you're creating a
document with lots of names or scientific terms, you may
want to turn off Spell-As-You-Go. To do so, open the Tools
menu and deselect Spell-As-You-Go. You can turn it back
on anytime.

USING THE SPELL CHECKER

You might prefer to turn off Spell-As-You-Go and use the Spell
Checker feature instead to check the document after you finish
typing. Follow these steps to run Spell Checker to check your
document:

1. Open the Tools menu and select Spell Check. Or, you can
   simply click the Spell Check button on the Toolbar. The
   Spell Checker dialog box appears, and Spell Checker begins checking your document.

Quick Spell To open Spell Checker from the
QuickMenu, right-click inside the document and select
Spell Check.

2. When Spell Checker encounters a word that is not in one
   of its dictionaries, it displays the word along with some
   possible replacements (see Figure 23.1). Respond to it in
   one of the following ways:

   • Select the correct spelling from the Replacements list
     and click Replace.

- Ask Spell Checker for additional choices by clicking Suggest.

- If Spell Checker is unable to provide a suggestion, type the correct spelling in the Replace with text box and click Replace.

- If the misspelling is a typing error you make often, click QuickCorrect to add it to the QuickCorrect list (see Lesson 5 for details).

- Click Skip Once to skip this occurrence of the word, or choose Skip Always to skip all occurrences of the word.

- Click Add to add the word to the dictionary.

- Click Undo to undo the most recent replacement.

- Click Customize to organize how Spell Checker checks your document.

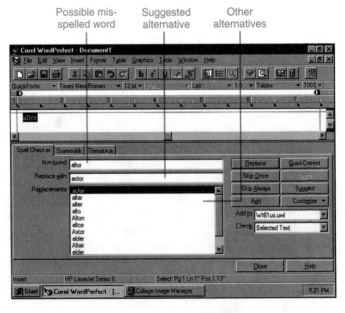

FIGURE 23.1 The Spell Checker dialog box.

3. (Optional) Click Close to exit Spell Checker at any time.

4. When Spell Checker finishes, click Yes to close it and return to your document.

Checking Your Grammar

WordPerfect contains a grammar checking program called Grammatik that can check your document for grammatical errors, incorrect punctuation, and improper word usage.

Follow these steps to activate Grammatik:

1. Open the Tools menu and select Grammatik. The Grammatik dialog box appears, and Grammatik begins checking your document.

2. When Grammatik encounters what it thinks is an error, it displays the error along with some possible replacements, as shown in Figure 23.2. Respond to it in one of the following ways:

   - Select the best alternative from the Replacements list and click Replace.

   - Click Skip Once to skip this occurrence of the error, or choose Skip Always to skip all occurrences of the error.

   - Click Turn Off to prevent Grammatik from stopping at similar errors.

   - If the error is a word you often type incorrectly, click QuickCorrect to add it to the QuickCorrect list (see Lesson 5).

   - Click Undo to undo the most recent correction.

   - Click Analysis to display an in-depth review of the error.

   - Click Customize to organize how Grammatik checks your document.

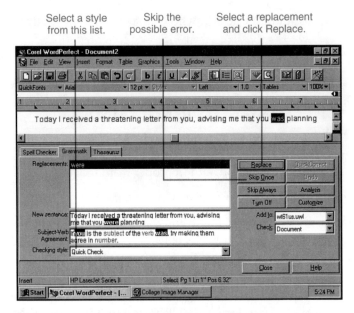

Select a style   Skip the   Select a replacement
from this list.   possible error.   and click Replace.

FIGURE 23.2   Grammatik looks for a wide range of errors and offers ways to correct them.

3. From the Checking style list, choose a checking style appropriate for your type of document. (You wouldn't want to check a fictional story using a "Very Strict" style, for example.)

4. (Optional) Click Close to exit Grammatik at any time.

5. When Grammatik finishes, click Yes to close Grammatik and return to your document.

USING THE THESAURUS

The Thesaurus can help you find the best word to use in your document. The WordPerfect Thesaurus offers synonyms (words that have similar meanings) for any selected word in your document. You can substitute any word in the Thesaurus for the original word. The following steps show you how to use the Thesaurus.

1. Position the cursor in the word whose synonyms you want to view. This word will become the *headword*.

 Headword   The word you're looking up. Each headword has its own list of synonyms .

2. Open the Tools menu and select Thesaurus. The Thesaurus dialog box appears, as shown in Figure 23.3. WordPerfect displays a list of synonyms for the headword.

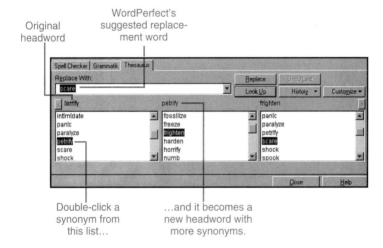

Original headword

WordPerfect's suggested replacement word

Double-click a synonym from this list…

…and it becomes a new headword with more synonyms.

FIGURE 23.3   The Thesaurus displays a list of synonyms for each selected word.

 Look One Up   While the Thesaurus is open, you can look up another word. Type a word in the Replace With text box and click Look Up. The Thesaurus displays a list of synonyms for the word you entered.

3. Respond to the Thesaurus in one of the following ways:

- Click Replace to substitute the word in the Replace With text box for the original word in your document.

- To view other words you have looked up, open the History list.

- Click Customize to organize how the Thesaurus looks up your words.

4. Click Close to return to your document. If you made a change with Thesaurus, WordPerfect implements that change.

Keep Looking   To expand the list of synonyms in the Thesaurus, double-click a word in the Synonym list. It becomes a new headword, and WordPerfect displays a list of synonyms for it in the next column to the right. You can then double-click a synonym from that list to create another new list. Expand the search until you find the best word for your document.

In this lesson, you learned how to use WordPerfect's writing tools to perfect your document. In the next lesson, you'll learn how to add graphic objects.

ADDING GRAPHIC OBJECTS TO YOUR DOCUMENT

In this lesson, you'll learn how to add pictures to your document. You'll also learn how to add lines, text boxes, and watermarks.

ADDING PICTURES TO YOUR DOCUMENT

Pictures, or *graphic images*, add visual impact to your document. By adding a picture, you can transform an ordinary page of text into a dramatic presentation.

You can add both *vector* and *bitmapped* graphic images to your document. WordPerfect places every picture in a graphics box. You can move or resize that box at any time.

Vector Graphics   Images created using line art, which have smooth edges.

Bitmapped Graphics   Images created using a series of dots, which have rough edges and look grainy.

WordPerfect comes with a number of graphic images. In addition, you can purchase many *clip art* packages that contain all types of pictures.

To add a graphic image to a WordPerfect document, follow these steps:

1. Position the cursor where you want the top left edge of the graphic to appear.

2. Open the Graphics menu and click Drag to Create if it's not already checked.

 3. Open the Graphics menu again and choose Image, or click the Image button on the Toolbar. Your mouse pointer changes to a hand holding a small dotted-line box.

4. Drag downward and to the right to draw a box in which you want the image placed (see Figure 24.1). When you release the mouse button, the Insert Image dialog box appears.

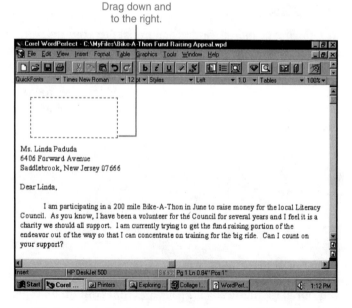

FIGURE 24.1   Draw the box where the image will be placed.

5. Change to the drive and folder that contain the graphic image you want to use. (WordPerfect comes with several graphic files, which are located in the COREL\OFFICE7\GRAPHICS folder.)

6. Click the name of the graphic image you want to use. If you want to preview graphic images before you insert them into your document, open the View menu and choose Preview and Content. (You only have to do this once to preview all graphic images.) The picture appears in the Viewer window, as shown in Figure 24.2.

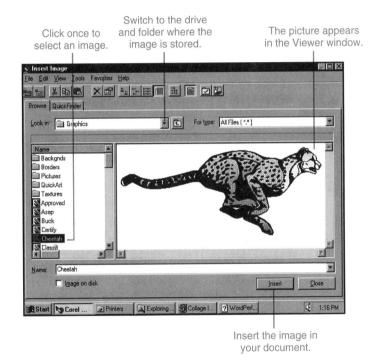

Click once to select an image.

Switch to the drive and folder where the image is stored.

The picture appears in the Viewer window.

Insert the image in your document.

FIGURE 24.2   You can view a graphic image before you place it in your document.

7. (Optional) Select another file name to see that image in the viewer.

8. Click Insert to insert the selected picture in the box you drew. WordPerfect places the picture (in the invisible box) in your document.

MOVING, RESIZING, OR DELETING A GRAPHICS BOX

If you want to move, resize, or delete a graphics box, click (select) it. Sizing handles (small black boxes) appear around the edges of a selected graphic. With the graphics box selected, move, delete, or resize it as described below:

Move   To move the image, place the mouse pointer inside the box. When the pointer changes to a four-headed arrow, drag the box to its new location and release the mouse button.

Resize   To resize the box, click a sizing handle and drag it to the desired size or dimension.

Delete   To delete a graphics box, press Delete.

When you finish editing a graphics box, click outside the box to deselect it.

 Right Image   Right-click a graphics box to access the **TIP** Graphics QuickMenu. Then experiment with some of the commands listed there.

ADDING A TEXT BOX

A text box is a graphics box that contains text. The advantage to using a text box is that you can position the box anywhere on a page. For example, placing a text box that contains the company name in the upper-left corner of a document could produce dramatic letterhead stationery.

You can create a text box by following these steps:

1. Position the cursor where you want the top left edge of the text box to appear.

2. Open the Graphics menu and click Drag to Create if it's not already checked.

3. Open the Graphics menu again and choose Text Box. Your mouse pointer changes to a hand holding a small dotted-line box.

4. Drag downward and to the right to draw the box in which you want the text placed.

5. Type the text into the box.

6. (Optional) Change the font style and size and add text attributes as desired.

Create a Text Box from the Toolbar   You can click the Text Box button on the Toolbar to create a text box. To make the button visible, drag the Toolbar into the document screen, or display two rows of Toolbar buttons. See Lesson 2 for details.

Change the Border Style   You can change the border style of a text box. To do so, right-click in the text box and choose Border/Fill from the QuickMenu. In the Box Border/Fill dialog box, select a new border style, and then click OK to implement the change and return to the document screen.

USING TEXTART

TextArt is a WordPerfect module that enables you to distort and modify text so it fits into various shapes. You can resize the text, add a shadow, and use borders and fills with TextArt.

WordPerfect inserts TextArt in your document in a graphics box, just as it does an image. Therefore, you can move, resize, and delete TextArt in the same way you would an image.

Follow these steps to have fun with TextArt:

1. Position the cursor where you want the upper-left edge of the TextArt box to appear.

2. Open the Graphics menu and choose TextArt. The TextArt 7 dialog box appears (see Figure 24.3).

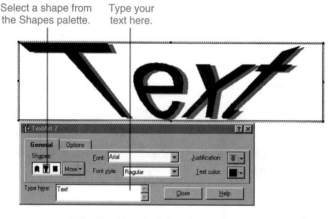

FIGURE 24.3   The TextArt 7 dialog box offers many choices for changing the appearance of text.

3. Type your text in the Type here box.

4. Select a shape from the Shapes palette.

5. (Optional) Change the text color and/or justification.

6. (Optional) Click the Options tab to change the pattern, shadow, outline, or smoothness, and/or to rotate the TextArt box.

7. Click Close to close the TextArt 7 dialog box and insert the TextArt box into your document.

Small Doses   You are limited to three lines of text (58 characters) in a TextArt box.

ADDING GRAPHIC LINES TO YOUR DOCUMENT

You can further enhance your document by adding vertical or horizontal lines. To add a graphic line to your document, follow these steps:

1. Position the cursor at the point you want the line to appear.

2. Open the Graphics menu and choose either Horizontal Line or Vertical Line. WordPerfect inserts a vertical or horizontal line in a default length, thickness, and style.

Line Fun To edit a line, click it once to select it, and then open the Graphics menu and select Edit Line. In the resulting dialog box, you can change the line style, length, position, color, and thickness.

Quick Lines Use QuickLines to create a horizontal line that extends from the left margin to the right margin. At the beginning of a line, type three hyphens (---) to insert a single line or type three equal signs (===) to insert a double line. Then press Enter, and the line appears in your document.

USING WATERMARKS

A *watermark* is a custom graphics box that prints in a lighter shade so that it appears as a background behind the text in your document. A watermark can include text or a graphic. Figure 24.4 shows a letter with a watermark.

You can add a watermark to every page or to selected pages. WordPerfect comes with many watermarks, but you can also use any text or graphic image to create your own.

Last on the List   Your best bet is to create a watermark after you've typed your document. When the watermark appears on-screen, text editing is considerably slower.

Watermark

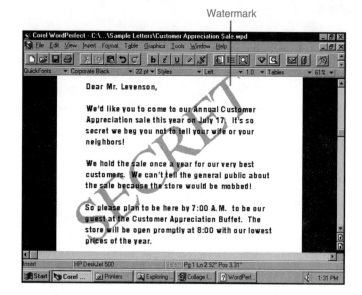

FIGURE 24.4   Add a watermark for a touch of class.

Follow these steps to create a watermark:

1. Position the cursor on the page where you want the watermark to appear.

2. Open the Format menu and choose Watermark.

 Fast Choice   You can bypass steps 1 and 2 by right-clicking at the top of the page and choosing Watermark from the QuickMenu.

3. If this is the first place in the document you're adding a watermark, choose Watermark A. If you have already added one watermark to the document, choose Watermark B to create a new one.

4. Click Create. The Watermark editing screen and the Watermark Feature Bar appear.

5. Click the Image button on the Watermark Feature Bar. The Insert Images dialog box appears (refer to Figure 24.2).

6. Select the image you want and click Insert. WordPerfect displays the selected image in the Watermark editing screen.

7. Click the Pages button on the Watermark Feature Bar and tell WordPerfect whether the watermark should appear on even or odd pages or every page. Then click OK.

8. Click Close to close the Watermark editing screen and add the watermark to your document.

You can discontinue a watermark anywhere in your document. With the cursor on the page where you want to stop it, select Format, Watermark, select Watermark A or Watermark B, and click Discontinue. WordPerfect removes the watermark from that page and all pages thereafter.

In this chapter, you learned the basics of working with graphic objects, lines, TextArt, and watermarks. In the next chapter, you'll learn about WordPerfect's Internet Publisher.

25 USING INTERNET PUBLISHER

In this lesson, you'll learn how to use WordPerfect's Internet Publisher to publish a document to the World Wide Web and view the document as others will see it.

WHAT IS THE INTERNET?

The Internet is a giant computer network that connects millions of computers together. By connecting to the Internet, government agencies, universities, corporations, special interest groups, and individuals like yourself can communicate with one another. Once you are connected to the Internet, you can access a number of resources stored on other computers. For example, you can copy files, send and receive electronic mail (e-mail), shop electronically, or read from several thousand publications.

The World Wide Web (also known as the Web or WWW) is a part of the Internet that consists of a collection of networks that allow you to browse through on-screen documents. These documents can be placed on the Web by anyone; small businesses, large corporations, individuals, and clubs all create *Web sites*.

When you are viewing one Web site, you can click a *hypertext link* to move quickly to another site. A hypertext link is usually a word that appears underlined or highlighted on the screen. You click a link to jump to a different page. By moving around via hypertext links, you can find many related and interesting documents.

In order to place a document on the Web, you must have a *modem* and an Internet service provider. The Internet provider grants you access to the Web and stores and maintains your Web site and documents. Because Internet providers generally charge a fee, you should shop around a bit before you sign up with one.

For more information on the Internet and how to connect to it, consult *Using the Internet* or *The Complete Idiot's Guide to the Internet*, also available from Que.

 Modem   A device connected to your computer that enables the computer to communicate with other computers by transferring computer data over ordinary phone lines.

If you want to take advantage of the resources of the Internet, you need to first get an Internet service provider. In addition, to view the Web, you must have special software called a *browser*. A very popular Web browser called Netscape Navigator is included with WordPerfect.

CREATING A WEB DOCUMENT

A document that is the main, default page of an individual or an organization on the Web is called a *home page*. You can create a home page that displays information about your business, for example.

The document you create for the Web must be created in HTML (HyperText Markup Language). When you create a Web document in WordPerfect, the Internet Publisher feature handles all of the translation to HTML. You use the Web Editor from WordPerfect's Internet Publisher to create and edit Web documents, publish those pages to HTML, retrieve an existing Web document, or create a document using a Web template.

Follow these steps to create a document using the Web Editor:

1. Open the File menu and choose Internet Publisher. The Internet Publisher dialog box appears (see Figure 25.1).

2. Click New Web Document. In the dialog box that appears, choose the Create a Blank Web Document template and click Select.

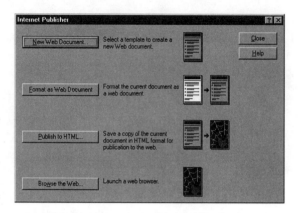

Figure 25.1　The Internet Publisher dialog box.

3. Read the message in the box shown in Figure 25.2 and click OK. The Web Editor opens. Notice that the menu bar, the Toolbar, and the Power Bar have changed.

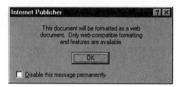

Figure 25.2　Click OK to continue.

4. Create your document. As you type, you can select different headings from the Font Size dialog box, as shown in Figure 25.3.

5. (Optional) Add headings, lists, tables, and so on to your Web page document.

6. When you finish the document, open the Format menu and choose Title. Because Web browsers display document titles instead of file names in the title bar, click Custom title and type a custom title, or click the First heading option button to use the first heading as the title for the document. Then click OK.

The Web Editor
Toolbar and Power Bar

Choose a heading
from the QuickFonts
drop-down list.

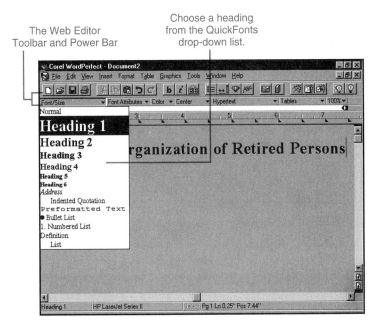

FIGURE 25.3   WordPerfect lets you create Web documents using the Web Editor.

7. Open the File menu and choose Save, or click the Save button on the Toolbar to save your document to disk in the normal manner.

TIP   **Sorry, Not Here**   The following WordPerfect features are not supported in HTML documents: columns, drop caps, page numbering, headers and footers, tabs and indents, watermarks, vertical lines, and fills (shading).

FORMATTING A WORDPERFECT DOCUMENT AS A WEB DOCUMENT

You can format an existing document for use on the Internet by following these steps:

1. Open the document you want to use.

2. Open the File menu and choose Internet Publisher. The Internet Publisher dialog box appears.

3. Choose Format as Web Document, and the Web Editor opens. (Notice that the menu bar, the Toolbar, and the Power Bar have changed.)

4. Follow steps 4–7 in the previous section to format, give a title to, and save your document.

To publish the document to HTML, skip down to the section "Publishing to HTML" (later in this lesson) and follow those steps.

VIEWING THE DOCUMENT IN HTML

Many people will have the opportunity to view your document on the WWW, so it's a good idea to see how your document will look on the WWW before you actually put it out on the Web site. You can view the document in Netscape at any time while you are working on it. Follow these steps to view your Web document as others will see it:

1. Perform steps 1–3 in the previous section to open a document in the Web Editor.

2. When the document is on-screen, open the View menu and choose View in Web Browser (or click the View in Web Browser button on the Web Editor Toolbar). Your document appears in Netscape. Figure 25.4 shows an example document displayed in a Web browser.

3. To close the Web browser and return to WordPerfect, click the Close (X) button at the right end of the title bar.

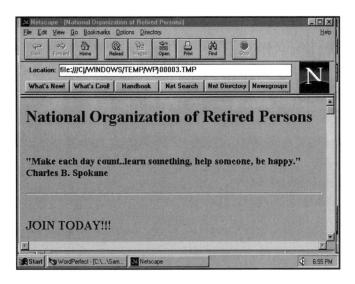

FIGURE 25.4   A Web document as viewed with a Web browser.

PUBLISHING TO HTML

Once you have viewed and saved a document using the Web Editor, you can publish it to HTML format. The Internet Publisher converts whatever codes or styles you added into HTML tags. Then it exports your document with the path and file name of the original Web document, but gives it an .HTM file extension.

With the document on-screen in the Web Editor, open the File menu, choose Internet Publisher, and select Publish to HTML (or simply click the Publish to HTML button on the Web Editor Toolbar). Click OK to save the document with the same name and path but with the .HTM file extension.

When you finish creating your HTML file, contact your Internet provider for instructions on how to place your page on the WWW.

LAUNCHING THE NETSCAPE NAVIGATOR BROWSER

You can launch Netscape Navigator directly from within WordPerfect at any time. First, follow the instructions furnished by your Internet provider to connect to the Internet. Then select File, Internet Publisher, Browse the Web, or click the Browse the Web button on the WordPerfect 7 Toolbar to open Netscape Navigator.

Now that you know how to create a Web document and put it on the Web, you might want to learn more about Netscape Navigator and everything that it makes available to you on the Internet. Pick up a copy of Que's *Netscape Navigator 6 in 1* to learn more about what you can do with this powerful browser.

In this lesson, you learned how to create and edit Web documents and how to view and publish them in HTML format. Congratulations! This is the last lesson, and you're well on your way to becoming a Corel WordPerfect expert!

INDEX

A

adding
    borders (columns), 126,
      139-142
    drop caps, 135-136
    fills (columns), 126
    graphics, 157-163
    items to numbered lists,
      120-121
    lines (columns), 126
    page numbers, 110-112
    text boxes to graphics
      boxes, 160-165
Address Book, 69-71
Address Book-Personal Information dialog box, 25
adjusting column width, 132
applying attributes (text),
  85-86
Ask the PerfectExpert feature
  (Help menu), 19-20

B

back tab, 100
balanced columns, 122
bars, see *individual bars*
binding option (printing),
  65-67

bitmapped graphics, 157
block protect (columns), 123
Border/Fill dialog box, 140
borders
    adding, 126, 139-142
    changing styles (text boxes),
      161
Box Border/Fill dialog box,
  161
browsers, Netscape Navigator,
  172
bulleted lists, creating,
  118-120
Bullets & Numbers dialog box,
  119
buttons
    Close, 1
    Display (PerfectExpert), 18
    in Windows Explorer, 53
    Line Spacing, 88
    Maximize, 1
    Minimize/Restore, 1
    New Blank Document, 22
    Power Bar, 10-11
    QuickFonts (Power Bar), 85
    Size to Fit, 132
    Toolbar, 9-10

C

Calculate dialog box, 134
cascading windows/menus, 57
cells (tables), 133-134

Center Page(s) dialog box, 139
centering text, 138-139
check marks, menu items, 6
clearing tabs, 93-94
Clipboard, 43
Close button, 1
codes, 75-77
    changing, 80
    hidden, revealing, 77-79,
      145-149
    open, 76
    page break codes, 113
    paired, 76
    removing, 79
    replacing, 146-149
    single, 76
columns, 122-123
    adding, 131
    adjusting width, 132
    balanced columns, 122
    borders, adding, 126
    column widths, 126
    defining, 124-126
    deleting, 131
    entering text into, 125-126
    fills, adding, 126
    lines, adding, 126
    newspaper columns, 122
    parallel columns, 122
    parallel columns with block
      protect, 123
    summing a table column,
      134
    turning off, 126
Columns dialog box, 124
commands
    dimmed commands, 6
    Edit menu, 42
    File menu, Save As, 48-50
    Help menu, 15
Contents tab (Help Topics
    screen), 16
controlling page breaks,
    112-113

Copy command (Edit menu),
    42
copying text blocks, 42-45
correcting mistakes
    (QuickCorrect), 33-36
Create Labels dialog box, 72
Create Table dialog box, 128
cursors, 2, 26
Cut command (Edit menu), 42

D

defaults
    fonts, changing, 83-84
    tab settings, 91, 96
defining columns, 124-126
deleting
    codes, 79
    text blocks, 42
dialog boxes, 12-14
    Address Book-Personal
      Information, 25
    Border/Fill, 140
    Box Border/Fill, 161
    Bullets & Numbers, 119
    Calculate, 134
    Center Page(s), 139
    Columns, 124
    Create Labels, 73
    Create Table, 128
    Document Initial Font, 83
    Edit Page Size, 106
    Envelope, 68
    Find and Replace Text, 143
    Font, 83
    Headers/Footers, 114
    Help Topics, 17
    Insert Columns/Rows, 131
    Labels, 71
    Line Spacing, 88
    New Entry, 25
    Open, 52
    Page Size, 105
    Paragraph Border/Fill, 141

Paragraph, 101
Print, 60-62
Properties, 26
Properties for Table
  Lines/Fill, 133
QuickCorrect, 35, 121
Save As, 46
Select New Document, 23
Select Page Numbering
  Format, 110
Tab Set, 94
TextArt 7, 162
Undo/Redo History, 38
Value/Adjust Number, 112
WordPerfect Characters, 138
dimmed commands, 6
Display button (PerfectExpert),
  18
displaying Toolbar buttons,
  multiple rows, 9-10
Do It for me option
  (PerfectExpert), 18
Document Initial Font dialog
  box, 83
document window, 2, 9
documents
  columns, defining, 124-126
  document window, 9
  entering text, 26-27
  finding, QuickFinder, 55-56
  formatting current
    document as Web
    document, 170
  graphics, adding, 157-163
  justification, changing,
    89-90
  navigating, 27-31
  opening
    existing documents,
      51-54
    from other programs,
      54-58

previewing (printing), 61-62
printing, 62-64
  binding option, 65-67
  options, 63
  preparing to print, 59-61
  previewing, 61-62
  order, reversing, 64
  troubleshooting, 64
  two-sided printing, 65-67
  publishing to HTML (Web
    documents), 171
  reformatting (Make it Fit),
    64-65
  saving, 46-50
  templates, creating with,
    23-26
  viewing multiple, 57-58
  viewing in HTML, 170-172
Draft mode, 30
drivers, 59
drop caps, adding, 135-136

E

Edit Page Size dialog box, 106
editing
  footers, 116-117
  headers, 116-117
  text, reversing changes,
    36-38
ellipsis, menu items, 6
Envelope dialog box, 68
envelopes, creating, Address
  Book, 68-71
exiting WordPerfect, 3

F

Favorites list, 53-54
Feature Bar (headers/footers),
  115

files
    closing, 50
    finding (QuickFinder),
        55-56
    opening, 53-58
    viewing multiple, 57-58
fills, 139
    adding to columns, 126
    changing (tables), 133
Find and Replace Text dialog
    box, 143
Find tab (Help Topics screen),
    17
finding
    documents (QuickFinder),
        55-56
    files (QuickFinder), 55-56
    text strings, 143-146
fixed width (columns), 125
Font dialog box, 83
fonts, 82-84
footers, 113-114
    creating, 114-116
    editing, 116-117
    Feature Bar, 115
    turning off, 117
    zeroing in, 114
formatting paragraphs,
    QuickFormat, 102-103

G

grammar checking
    (Grammatik), 153-154
graphics
    adding, 157-161
    bitmapped, 157
    boxes
        adding text boxes,
            160-165
        manipulating, 160
        watermarks, 163-165
    lines, adding to documents,
        163
    vector, 157

Guide Me through it option
    (PerfectExpert), 18
Guidelines, 3

H

headers, 113-114
    creating, 114-116
    editing, 116-117
    Feature Bar, 115
    turning off, 117
    zeroing in, 114
Headers/Footers dialog
    box, 114
headword (Thesaurus), 155
Help, F1 key (Help screen), 19
Help menu, 15
    Ask the PerfectExpert
        feature, 19-20
    commands, 15
    Help Topics screen, 16-19
    QuickTips, 20-21
Help Topics dialog box, 17
Help Topics screen, 16-19
    Contents tab, 16
    Find tab, 17
    Index tab, 16
    Show Me tab, 17-21
hidden codes
    revealing, 77-79
    searching for, 145-149
hiding
    Power Bar, 12
    Ruler Bar, 12
    Toolbars, 9
highlights, borders, 142

I

indenting text, 99-100
Index tab (Help Topics screen),
    16
Insert Columns/Rows dialog
    box, 131

Insert mode, 32
inserting text, 32
Internet Publisher, Web documents
  creating, 167-171
  formatting current document as a Web document, 170
  launching Netscape Navigator, 172
  publishing to HTML, 171
  viewing in HTML, 170-172

J-L

justification changing, 88-90
labels
  creating, 71-74
  label definitions, creating, 71-73
  printing, 73-74
  typing, 73-74
Labels dialog box, 71
leaders (tab stops), 93
line spacing, changing, 87-88
Line Spacing Button, 88
Line Spacing dialog box, 88
lines
  adding to columns, 126
  changing (tables), 133
lists
  adding and removing items, 120-121
  creating, 118-120

M

Make It Fit utility, reformatting documents, 64-65
Maximize button, 1
Menu bar, 2, 5-7

minimizing windows, 4
Minimize/Restore button, 1
mistakes, correcting (QuickCorrect), 33-36
modules, TextArt, 161-162
mouse, navigating documents, 28-31
moving
  text within tables, 129-130
  text blocks, 42-45
  Toolbars, 8-14
My Addresses tab, 25

N-O

Netscape Navigator browser, launching, 172
New Blank Document button, 22
New Entry dialog box, 25
newspaper columns, 122
numbered lists, creating, 118-120
numbers options, 134

open codes, 76
Open dialog box, 52
open styles, 80
opening
  documents
    existing, 51-54
    from other programs, 54-58
  files
    from other programs, 54-58
    with Favorites, 53-54

P

page breaks, controlling, 112-113
page definitions, 104
page margins, setting, 107-109

Page mode, 30
page size, selecting, 104-107
Page Size dialog box, 105
page sizes, changing, 106-109
pagination, adding, 110-113
pages
    breaks, controlling, 112-113
    definitions, 104
    footers, 113-117
    headers, 113-117
    size, selecting, 104-107
paired codes, 76
Paragraph Border/Fill dialog
    box, 141
Paragraph dialog box, 101
paragraphs
    borders, 141
    characteristics, 98
    formatting (QuickFormat),
      102-103
    indents, 99-100
    QuickSpots, 101
parallel columns, 122-123
Paste command (Edit menu), 42
PerfectExpert (Help menu,
    Show Me tab), 17-18
personal information
    (template), 25-27
Play a Demo option
    (PerfectExpert), 17
Power Bar, 2, 10-12, 85-86
power justification, 90
Previewer window (creating
    documents), 24
previewing documents (print-
    ing), 61-62
Print dialog box, 60, 62
printer dependent page
    definitions, 104
Printer tab, 60
printing
    documents, 62-64
      binding option, 65-67
      preparing, 59-61
      previewing, 61-62

      reversing print order, 64
      troubleshooting, 64
      two-sided printing, 65-67
    labels, 73-74
Properties dialog box, 26
Properties for Table Lines/Fill
    dialog box, 133

Q

Quick Characters, WordPerfect
    characters, 138
QuickCorrect (correcting
    mistakes), 34-38, 121
QuickFinder (finding
    documents and files), 55-56
QuickFonts button (Power
    bar), 85
QuickFormat (formatting
    paragraphs), 102-103
QuickMenu, 100, 120, 129
QuickSpots (paragraph
    options), 101
QuickTips command (Help
    menu), 20-21

R

reformatting documents,
    64-65
removing
    codes, 79
    items, numbered lists,
      120-121
replacing text, 146-149
revealing hidden codes, 77-79
right arrows, menu items, 6
rows, adding or deleting in
    tables, 131-132
Ruler Bar, 11-12, 124
    hiding, 12
    setting page margins, 109
    tab settings, changing 97

S

Save As command, 48-50
Save As dialog box, 46
saving documents, 46-50
screens, 1-3
    Document screen, 2
    Help Topics, 16-19
    views, changing, 30-31
    WYSIWYG (what-you-see-is-
        what-you-get), 31
scroll bars, 3, 28-31
scrolling documents, 28-31
searching, hidden codes,
    145-149
Select New Document dialog
    box, 23
Select Page Numbering Format
    dialog box, 110
Select template list, 24
selecting
    label definitions, 71-72
    page size, 104-107
    text blocks, 39-41
setting
    page margins, 107-109
    tabs, 92-97
shadow pointer, 26
shortcuts
    changing font sizes, 83
    menu bar, 6
    opening files, 53-54
    Printer tab, 60
Show Me tab (Help Topics
    screen), 17-21
single codes, 76
Size to Fit button (columns),
    132
sizes, tables, changing,
    130-134
spacing tabs, 96
special characters, 137-138
SpeedFormat (table sizing),
    130
Spell Checker, 150-156

Spell-As-You-Go, 150-151
Status Bar, 3
strings, text, finding, 143-146
styles (templates), 24
switching Toolbars, 8
synonyms, Thesaurus, 154-156

T

Tab Set dialog box, 94
Table QuickMenu, 129
tables, 127-128
    creating, 128-129
    moving text within,
        129-130
    numbers options, 134
    size, changing, 130-134
    summing a column, 134
    typing text within, 129-130
tabs, 91
    absolute, 91
    back tab, 100
    Contents tab (Help Topics
        screen), 16, 17
    default settings, 91
    My Addresses tab, 25
    relative, 91
    settings, changing, 94-97
    Show Me tab (Help Topics
        screen), 17-21
    stops, 92-93
taskbar (Windows 95), 3
templates, 23-27
text
    attributes, applying, 85-86
    attributes, changing, 82-83
    boxes
        adding to graphics boxes,
          160-165
        changing border style,
          161
    centering, 138-139
    correcting mistakes
        (QuickCorrect), 33-38

editing, reversing changes, 36-38
entering, 26-27, 125-126
font sizes, 82-83
inserting, 32
moving within tables, 129-130
replacing, 146-149
strings, finding, 143-146
typing over, 32-33
text blocks
copying, 42-45
deleting, 42
moving, 42-45
selecting, 39-41
TextArt 7 dialog box, 162
TextArt module, 161-162
Thesaurus, 154-156
Toolbars, 2, 7-10
applying attributes (text), 85-86
buttons, 7-10
hiding, 9
indenting from, 100
moving, 8-14
switching, 8
troubleshooting, printing, 64
turning off
columns, 126
footers, 117
headers, 117
two page mode (changing screen view), 31
two-sided printing, 65-67
Typeover mode, 33
typing
labels, 73-74
over existing text, 32-33
text within tables, 129-130

U-Z

Undo Redo command (Edit menu), 36
Undo/Redo History dialog box, 38

Value/Adjust Number dialog box, 112
vector graphics, 157
viewing
documents in HTML, 57-58, 170-172
files, multiple, 57-58

watermarks (graphics boxes), 163-165
Web documents
creating (Internet Publisher), 167-171
formatting current documents as Web documents, 170
launching Netscape Navigator, 172
publishing to HTML, 171
viewing in HTML, 170-172
What You See Is What You Get, see *WYSIWYG*
wild cards, 55
windows
cascading, 57
document window, 9
Previewer window, 24
Windows 95 taskbar, 3
Windows Explorer, 53
word-wrap feature, 26
WordPerfect, exiting, 3
WordPerfect characters, see *special characters*
WordPerfect Characters dialog box, 138
WYSIWYG (what you see is what you get), 31

zooming, 62

Complete and Return this Card
for a *FREE* Computer Book Catalog

Thank you for purchasing this book! You have purchased a
superior computer book written expressly for your needs. To
continue to provide the kind of up-to-date, pertinent coverage
you've come to expect from us, we need to hear from you.
Please take a minute to complete and return this self-addressed,
postage-paid form. In return, we'll send you a free catalog of all
our computer books on topics ranging from word processing to
programming and the internet.

Mr. ☐   Mrs. ☐   Ms. ☐   Dr. ☐

Name (first) ☐☐☐☐☐☐☐☐☐☐ (M.I.) ☐ (last) ☐☐☐☐☐☐☐☐☐☐☐☐

Address ☐☐☐☐☐☐☐☐☐☐☐☐☐☐☐☐☐☐☐☐☐☐☐☐

☐☐☐☐☐☐☐☐☐☐☐☐☐☐☐☐☐☐☐☐☐☐☐☐

City ☐☐☐☐☐☐☐☐☐☐☐ State ☐☐ Zip ☐☐☐☐☐ ☐☐☐☐

Phone ☐☐☐ ☐☐☐ ☐☐☐☐ Fax ☐☐☐ ☐☐☐ ☐☐☐☐

Company Name ☐☐☐☐☐☐☐☐☐☐☐☐☐☐☐☐☐☐☐☐☐☐☐

E-mail address ☐☐☐☐☐☐☐☐☐☐☐☐☐☐☐☐☐☐☐☐☐☐☐

**1. Please check at least (3)
influencing factors for
purchasing this book.**

Front or back cover information on book .... ☐
Special approach to the content .... ☐
Completeness of content .... ☐
Author's reputation .... ☐
Publisher's reputation .... ☐
Book cover design or layout .... ☐
Index or table of contents of book .... ☐
Price of book .... ☐
Special effects, graphics, illustrations .... ☐
Other (Please specify): _____ ☐

**2. How did you first learn
about this book?**

Internet Site .... ☐
Saw in Macmillan Computer
Publishing catalog .... ☐
Recommended by store personnel .... ☐
Saw the book on bookshelf at store .... ☐
Recommended by a friend .... ☐
Received advertisement in the mail .... ☐
Saw an advertisement in: _____ ☐
Read book review in: _____ ☐
Other (Please specify): _____ ☐

**3. How many computer books have
you purchased in the last six
months?**

This book only .... ☐   3 to 5 books .... ☐
2 books .... ☐   More than 5 .... ☐

4. Where did you purchase this book?

Bookstore .... ☐
Computer Store .... ☐
Consumer Electronics Store .... ☐
Department Store .... ☐
Office Club .... ☐
Warehouse Club .... ☐
Mail Order .... ☐
Direct from Publisher .... ☐
Internet site .... ☐
Other (Please specify): .... ☐

**5. How long have you been using a
computer?**

Less than 6 months .. ☐   6 months to a year ..... ☐
1 to 3 years .... ☐   More than 3 years ...... ☐

**6. What is your level of experience with
personal computers and with the
subject of this book?**

	With PC's	With subject of book
New	☐	☐
Casual	☐	☐
Accomplished	☐	☐
Expert	☐	☐

Source Code — ISBN: 0-7897-454-4

7. Which of the following best describes your job title?

Administrative Assistant ☐
Coordinator ☐
Manager/Supervisor ☐
Director ☐
Vice President ☐
President/CEO/COO ☐
Lawyer/Doctor/Medical Professional ☐
Teacher/Educator/Trainer ☐
Engineer/Technician ☐
Consultant ☐
Not employed/Student/Retired ☐
Other (Please specify): ☐

8. Which of the following best describes the area of the company your job title falls under?

Accounting ☐
Engineering ☐
Manufacturing ☐
Marketing ☐
Operations ☐
Sales ☐
Other (Please specify): ☐

9. What is your age?

Under 20 ☐
21-29 ☐
30-39 ☐
40-49 ☐
50-59 ☐
60-over ☐

10. Are you:

Male ☐
Female ☐

11. Which computer publications do you read regularly? (Please list)

_____
_____
_____
_____
_____
_____
_____
_____
_____
_____

Comments: _____
_____
_____

Fold here and scotch-tape to